Amphoto Guide to
Travel Photography

Amphoto Guide to
Travel Photography

Bob Mitchell

AMPHOTO
American Photographic Book Publishing Co., Inc.
New York, New York

Note: In the appendix of this book, you will find a table for converting U.S. Customary measurements to the metric system. You will also find a table for ASA and DIN equivalents.

To Marilyn – who stayed home.

All photos in this book were taken by the author, using Konica cameras.

Library of Congress Cataloging in Publication Data
Mitchell, Bob
    Amphoto guide to travel photography.

    Includes index.
    1. Travel photography.   I. Title.
TR790.M57   778.9′9′91   79-18215

ISBN 0-8174-2472-5 (hardbound)
ISBN 0-8174-2144-0 (softbound)

Manufactured in the United States of America

OTHER BOOKS IN THE AMPHOTO GUIDE SERIES

Available now

Amphoto Guide to Basic Photography
Amphoto Guide to Black-and-White Processing and Printing
Amphoto Guide to Cameras
Amphoto Guide to Filters
Amphoto Guide to Lighting
Amphoto Guide to Photographing Models
Amphoto Guide to Selling Photographs: Rates & Rights

To be published

Amphoto Guide to Available Light Photography
Amphoto Guide to Darkroom Special Effects
Amphoto Guide to Non-Silver Processes

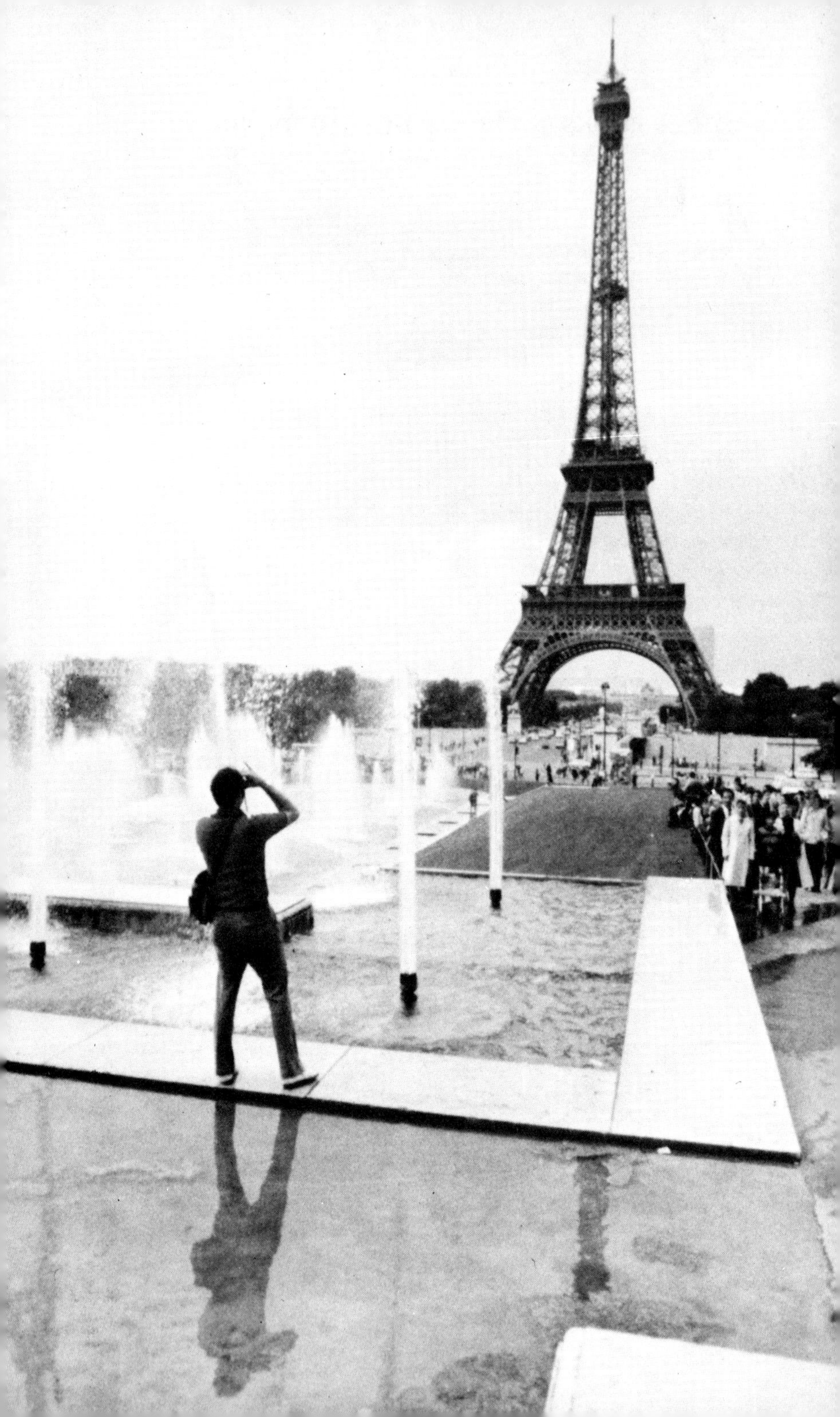

Contents

1	Your Trip—The Three Phases	9
2	The Plan	11
3	Off You Go	33
4	How to Shoot Travel Pictures	39
5	What to Shoot on Your Trip	57
6	Home Again	151
	Appendix	157
	Index	159

1

Your Trip—The Three Phases

There's a lot more to travel photography than just going someplace with your camera and getting home. Anybody can do that. What you want is to derive the maximum amount of pleasure from your trip—and come home with first class pictures as well.

Every overseas trip has three distinct phases: getting ready; making the trip itself; and looking back on the trip through pictures so it may be enjoyed all over again—and again and again.

Obviously, the most important part of planning your trip involves deciding where to go. Study any maps and brochures you can get on the area you have chosen to visit. Make lists of places to see and photograph at each stop on your itinerary. If you have friends who have already been where you are going, ask them for more information. Finally, pack your lightest possible kit of photographic gear, decide which and how much film to carry—and you're ready to go.

While you may expect the main phase of the trip—the actual going there and seeing and photographing it all—to be the best part, the looking-back phase may be even better.

Remembering your trip is a lasting thing that nobody can take away from you. When you begin developing all those pictures you shot on your trip, you'll relive each experience as though it just happened. The finished pictures will give you the opportunity to share the fun of it all with your friends at home. That first look at the newly processed pictures of the trip is as much a thrill for the most experienced shooter as for the brand new amateur.

2

The Plan

HOMEWORK

Even if you're no longer in school, you still have to do your homework. The only way to be ready for your trip is to read heavily and take copious notes.

First, sketch out an itinerary for your travels. List the major places you want to visit and, perhaps with the help of a travel agency, begin to map out a basic plan. A regular airline ticket allows you to make two stops on the way to your ultimate destination and two on the way back. By taking advantage of this, you can fly to five places free and make shorter side trips from each of these. Thus you can make the best use of your travel price.

Having outlined an itinerary, go to the library to begin your research on places you will visit. Look up every possible subject in your trip file. As you can't carry many books with you on your trip, make notes you can take along.

Before you leave the library, study all the photographs you can find of places you will visit. Some of these shots might be especially exciting. Ask yourself why you like these particular pictures. Is it the lighting? Is it the angle the photographer has chosen? Did he use special camera equipment such as a wide-angle or telephoto lens? Perhaps you were impressed by his use of a high angle for the best possible effect. Do you see anything in any of the pictures that you think you might do better by making a slight change of angle, of lighting, or of equipment? Try to remember all this when you're on your trip so you can improve on the picture you saw in the library. You might want to make sketches of some of the best pictures—for future approximation or improvements.

Has anyone you know visited any of the stops on your planned itinerary? Discuss their trip with them, making notes as you talk. No doubt they will be able to suggest all sorts of places to go and things to photograph. Furthermore, they may have good suggestions on where to sleep inexpensively and eat well.

Lists

While you're doing your homework, begin to make little lists. Use 3″ × 5″ file cards, which are easily carried in pocket or purse. Cards are better than notebooks, as they can be kept together with a rubber band, or sorted, shuffled, and edited as you go along, carrying only those pertinent to the day's business. Keep the currently most important card on the top of the stack. Don't throw away the used cards; these discarded notes will be a great help in going over your trip upon your return.

For every stop in your travels, have a list of places to see and photograph, along with the ideal time of day to do so. Keep some of the sketches you made of the photos in the library. Then, at the scene, you may have a fairly precise idea of how you will want to photograph it yourself.

Also make lists of good shopping stops, eating places, free entertainment, good theatres, concerts, and other points of interest. While much of this can be done on arrival, it is a good idea to have some preliminary general plans.

Shopping lists for each stop on your tour should be built up too. Travel brochures will supply you with good information about the shopping at each stop. All this data can be compressed onto a 3″ × 5″ card to which you can refer each evening for the next day's plan.

Rainy Day Planning

Without a doubt, some of your trip days are going to be rainy. Expect it and make your plans accordingly. You know there are indoor places you want to see and this is the time to do it. Remember, there is no point in shooting pictures in a museum while it is a nice sunny day outside!

On 3″ × 5″ cards, make a "rain list" for each city you expect to visit. This will include addresses of museums, galleries, department stores, bookstores, factories that provide guided tours, sightseeing tours, and more. When the weather turns rainy, take out your list.

Here, for example, is a rain list for London:

Albert Hall (concerts)	BBC Studios
British Museum	Covent Garden (Royal Opera)
Burlington Arcade	
Design Centre (new British products)	Foyle's Bookstore (world's largest)
Earl's Court Exhibition Hall	Imperial War Museum
Hampton Court Palace	National Film Theatre
Leadenhall Market	The Old Vic (theatre)
National Gallery	Festival Hall (concerts)
National Portrait Gallery	Science Museum
The Old Bailey (court)	Paddington Station
Royal Exchange	Victoria & Albert Museum
St. Paul's Cathedral	Westminster Abbey
Wallace Collection	Westminster Cathedral
	Tate Gallery

Itinerary and Time Schedule

When you have settled upon the major cities you want to visit, you should be able to begin to firm up your itinerary with a route and time schedule.

On one of your little 3″ × 5″ cards, make up a special calendar as shown in the accompanying illustration. Showing only those dates for your trip and the few days before and after, it has space for you to write in little notes about what you do on each day, where you go, and so forth. This will be your picture of your trip that you can update each day. At a glance, you can tell how many days remain of your trip and how your film supply is holding up.

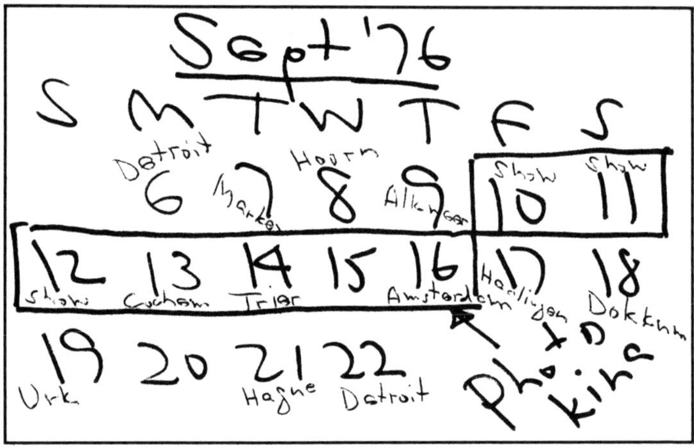

This mini calendar will be a great reference back home for years to come. We have a stack of such cards, each representing one of the trips of the past.

If your vacation allows three weeks, you first must take off a day at each end of the trip for getting there and back; this already drops your total number of days from 21 to 19.

Let's say that you have selected five major stops on your trip—your ultimate destination (the furthest point on your ticket) plus two stops getting there and two stops on the return leg. This means that you will also be using four more days—or at least parts of four more days—for travel. Now you're down to fifteen days that are not at least partly to be used for travel.

But—looking at your notes, you find that three of these five cities will require more time each than the remaining two cities. Therefore, you should plan to spend four days in each of the three cities and only three days total for the other two. Think in terms of days per city—not just how many cities.

Reservations

As soon as you know when you can leave and have a definite trip plan worked out, make your reservations through your travel agent or directly through an airline. The type of ticket we have described with the two stops going and two stops return is called a 14–21 day excursion ticket. It costs a little more than a non-stop tourist fare, but is well worth it.

One way to save a couple of shooting days from the travel days is to make as many as possible of the short legs of your trip in the evening or in the early morning. This way, you won't spend the best parts of those days sitting in airport terminals. For example, let's say you have just finished a good day of walking and picture shooting in Paris. You have a nice dinner in your favorite little restaurant, and then head out to the airport for your evening flight to Munich. Having made hotel reservations ahead of time, you arrive after a short jet flight and check into your hotel for the night. The next morning, you're all rested and ready to go once more.

PACKING

Weeks before you plan to leave, pack your suitcase and your camera bag with everything you expect to take with you. Weigh it all and then begin to discard what you can. From then on, add only those few items that you absolutely must. When this phase is completed, begin to cut your total luggage down by replacing each item with something smaller and lighter. Trim that shaving kit down to a small battery-powered razor or, even better, a safety razor; take a curling iron instead of a set of electric rollers; transfer all liquids to small plastic bottles, and so on. Before long, this will become a game and you will find yourself trying to pack the ultimate lightweight kit.

Most Sunday newspaper travel sections frequently run articles on how to pack your clothes for minimum weight and space. Pay attention to these articles, for your suitcase is a big part of the total baggage weight you must carry around with you. International air carriers allow you to take two pieces of luggage that will go in the baggage compartment and whatever hand luggage will fit comfortably under your seat. Remember that this is a *maximum* amount of luggage; the wise traveler carries as little as possible.

Save things on your trip only when you need them. Be ruthless on this point. One photographer once traveled to Japan for three weeks with 13 pounds of luggage, including 130 rolls of film, two cameras, four lenses, changes of shirts, ties, underwear, socks, and many little packets of detergent for nightly hand laundering. When other passengers were struggling with their huge suitcases (plural), this individual walked off the plane carrying camera bag and a single flight bag with shoulder strap.

Camera Equipment

While you're doing your planning, start to think about the photo kit you'll be taking along. Now is the time to ask yourself some basic questions. The answers to these questions will help you determine just which gear to take with you and which to leave at home.

The first thing you must decide is whether you will be taking movies or stills. Either will be just fine, but don't try to do both. Either one will require your full-time attention and if you try to do both each kind of shooting will suffer. Next, decide whether to shoot black-and-white or color. Again, shooting both will require your divided attention and both will suffer. Finally, decide whether you will want slides or prints. Concentrate on one facet of photography (such as color slides) and do the best job you know how. Don't try to do two things well at the same time.

When choosing what equipment to take along, first ask yourself which camera gear you find most comfortable to use and carry. Some photographers have worked with a twin-lens 6 × 6 cm camera for years and find this to be the only really comfortable size and format for them. Should such a person decide at the last minute to switch to a 35 mm SLR camera with a kit of lenses, he would be absolutely lost when he tried to work smoothly on the trip.

When you have outlined to yourself exactly what gear you want to take, ask yourself if you can carry it all with ease. Don't count on finding a porter wherever you travel. Remember that your camera gear is only a *part* of your whole outfit. Undoubtedly you will also be taking at least one suitcase with clothes and personal effects. Add this to your camera bag and the weight of your extra film and camera accessories and you will see why the camera and equipment part of your total luggage must be kept to a minimum.

Brand New Camera—Never. Whatever you do, don't go out and buy yourself a new camera for your trip and expect to come home with worthwhile pictures. Too many times, people purchase a brand new camera with all the latest features and forget to shoot a few rolls of film with it—and have the pictures processed. When they return home from the trip of a lifetime, they find that the shutter wasn't working properly and all of their wonderful shots were underexposed by a couple of *f*-stops. This is pretty funny unless it happens to you.

Your camera should be so familiar to you that you can work with it automatically—and know that it is doing the job you expect it to do. Working with your camera

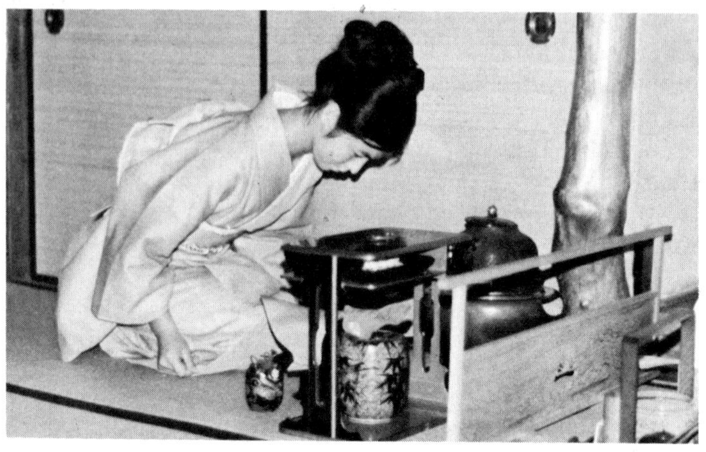

Here is one occasion where a little portable electronic flash allowed lighting for a subject that otherwise could not have been recorded. The traditional Japanese Tea Ceremony was poorly lighted but most interesting. Bounce flash would have been better, but was not possible with the available equipment. Taken with a 50 mm lens; 1/125 sec. at f/5.6.

should be like driving a car. You are thinking all the time, but you are driving automatically. Allow yourself a couple of months to become accustomed to a new camera for your trip. If it doesn't feel right, leave it behind and take your old camera instead.

Packing Your Camera Gear

If you've never made a trip abroad, you will be glad for any special planning you have done to make carrying and using your camera easy.

First, list precisely which camera or cameras you will be carrying with you—plus each lens plus every accessory you expect to take. This includes small electronic flash, tripod, filters, and the like. Also, how much film will you need each day and how much film in total?

Carrying Your Gear

Having decided on equipment and amount of film, you can begin to work out a simple means for carrying it all. Two different carrying situations must be considered. First, you must work out a good way to carry your kit when you are actually walking around shooting pictures. Second, you must remember that everything photographic that goes on your trip isn't in that walking-around kit. Only sometimes will you want your tripod with you. The same goes for your little strobe, and you certainly won't want to carry all of your film with you all the time.

Your walking-around photo kit might consist of one 35 mm camera with normal, telephoto, and wide-angle lenses; eight rolls of film; small strobe; small folding tripod; cable release; assorted filters; and your 3″ × 5″ note cards. All this can be fitted into a single gadget bag—except for the camera. The camera won't do you any good in there, so don't plan space for it. It belongs on a neck strap around your neck, where it can be called upon in an instant for that great candid shot.

How Much Film? One formula that always seems to work out just right is five 35 mm 36-exposure rolls per day for each day not spent traveling. Some days you will exceed this average and on others you will fall short, of course, but this rule has always worked out.

Remember, too, that film is widely available in most of the civilized world, although prices may vary and you may have extra processing costs. Unless you're planning to spend your entire trip in some very remote area, you should be able to purchase familiar brands of film almost anywhere.

Special Film Shoulder Bag. Most of the time, your extra film will remain in your suitcase in the hotel. But, when you travel, it should go into a small, hand-carried, fold-up vinyl bag. You should hand-carry your film through every airport terminal. Such a bag can be easily opened for customs inspection and will fit easily under your seat on the plane beside your regular camera bag.

Little fold-up vinyl zipper shoulder bags can be purchased in the photo departments of most stores. Such a bag will hold a lot of equipment, both photographic and otherwise. It is excellent for carrying your total supply of film for the trip onto the plane and on buses or trains. It greatly simplifies going through security checks and customs, because once it is unzipped, all the contents are immediately accessible. The shoulder strap assures that you have it all with you all the time.

Many of these bags also have room for magazines, candy bars, cigars, tape recorders, and all of the other little items that you want to have with you in transit. Even a small shaving kit can be carried in it, for freshening up on the plane.

Outfitting Your Gadget Bag. In order to carry your walking-around photo kit, you should make some sort of an insert for your gadget bag. Then, you can get at each piece of equipment immediately, when you need it, without any fumbling. Yours should be fitted to your needs and should not be a copy of what is shown in the photos on the next pages. The way you work with your camera should dictate how your kit is fitted so you will be able to work easily. This is a perfect illustration of the old saw: a place for everything and everything in its place.

To make the bag insert, place your lenses, film, and other accessories on a table with the bag nearby. Now arrange the lenses—front end down—so that they will cover no more than the length and width of the inside dimensions of the bag. (If they won't fit into the bag, perhaps you should leave one of them home and lighten the load. Or, you can go out and find a slightly larger bag. If you do, look for a used bag and not a new one. Old bags don't attract the attention of thieves as much as new ones.) *All* your lenses should be positioned in this layout—even the one that is usually on your camera. The reason for positioning the on-the-camera lens is because when you want to change lenses, you first remove whichever lens is on your camera and put it away in its place in the bag. Then, you select the lens you want to use next. It'll be there waiting for you in just the right place—and well protected. Since you're going to handle only one lens at a time, all this can be done with one hand.

With your lenses and other items all laid out, you will note that none are the same height. The tallest—your telephoto—should not be as tall as the inside of your bag. Next, make little cardboard boxes of various heights to fit under each item so that the lenses are all level and will just fit within the height of the bag. Cut a circular hole in the top of each box that will hold a lens, so the rear flange of the lens will project into the box and be protected from damage. When the top of your bag is closed, it will lie nicely on each piece of gear to hold it in place.

(The little boxes should be made of cardboard and held together with Elmer's Glue; they are only temporary, until you work out the finished insert for the bag. With all boxes in place and the lenses and other items positioned, you can check to see if all measurements are right. If not, remake whatever is necessary.)

Having made these preliminary boxes, stick them together for a final assembly so that you have a single integral unit. Check the unit out again to be sure it can be easily installed and that all pieces fit into the bag with the lid closed.

At this point, you will probably note that there is a lot of wasted and inaccessible space beneath the lens-holding insert. By redesigning the insert, you can work out some means of getting into this area, which is ideal for storing extra film rolls, repair tools, or accessories which you seldom use but don't want to leave behind. When you have figured out just how you're going to work this out, make your final insert, this time out of thin corrugated box material, gluing all pieces together with Elmer's Glue and reinforcing all corners with folded paper, gummed tape, or Scotch vinyl tape.

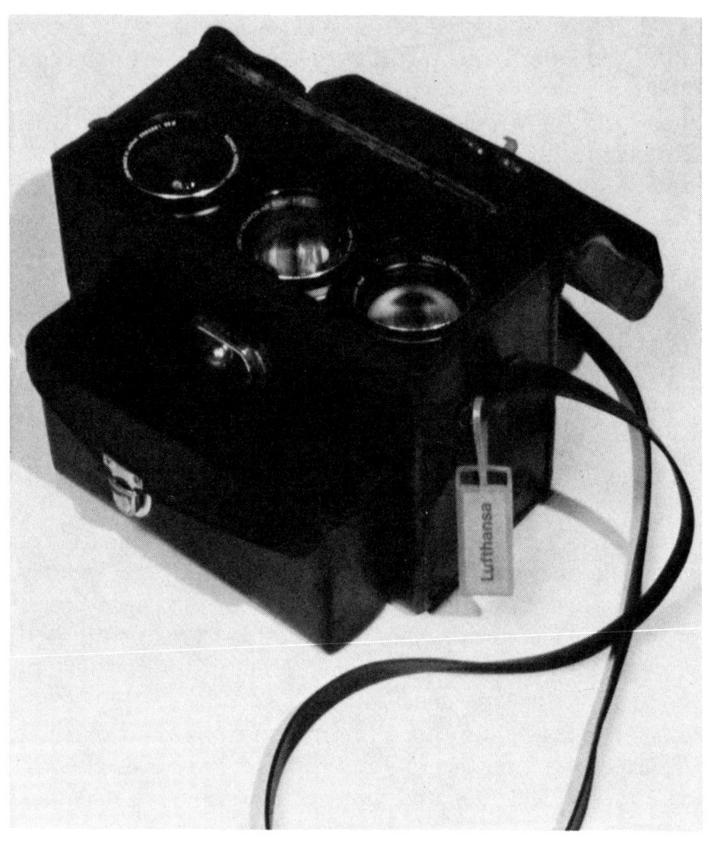

*Small camera bag outfitted to hold three lenses, a day's
supply of film, and a few additional accessories. When the
top of the bag is closed, all lenses are held tightly in position.*

One of the camera bags outfitted in the accompanying photos was fitted for three lenses for a Konica SLR.
They are the 24 mm, 50 mm, and 135 mm lenses with
automatic fittings at the rear. Note that these fittings and
the bayonet mounts project through holes provided in the
case. Two of the lenses are essentially the same length, so
they are placed on a common surface or deck. This deck is

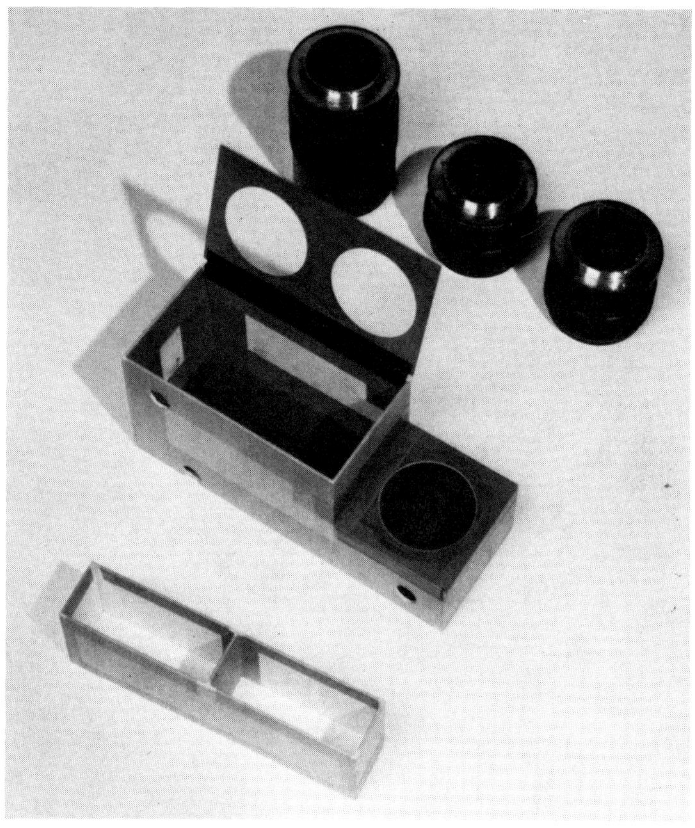

Insert for the small bag in opposite photo, removed to show its construction. Note that the top piece has been hinged with vinyl tape so that the area beneath is accessible for more storage of camera fittings such as small electronic flash, filters, etc.

hinged so that the space beneath is accessible from above when the lenses are removed. As the space beneath the third lens is also a part of this hidden area, nearly the entire bottom of the case is usable for extra storage. This case holds the following items: three lenses, nine rolls of film, kit of repair tools, pocket tripod, cable release, and a selection of filters. There is also a space in the back for

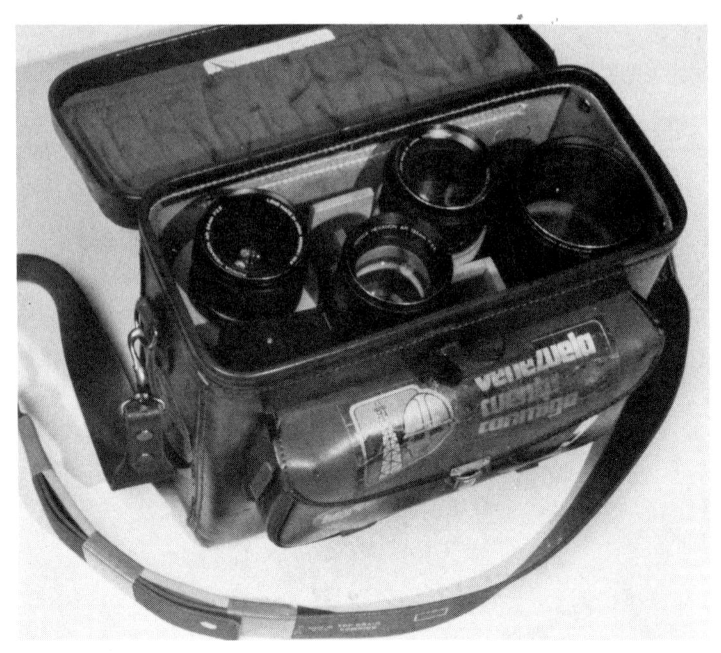

A large camera bag fitted with insert. Insert holds four lenses, electronic flash, and many other small items.

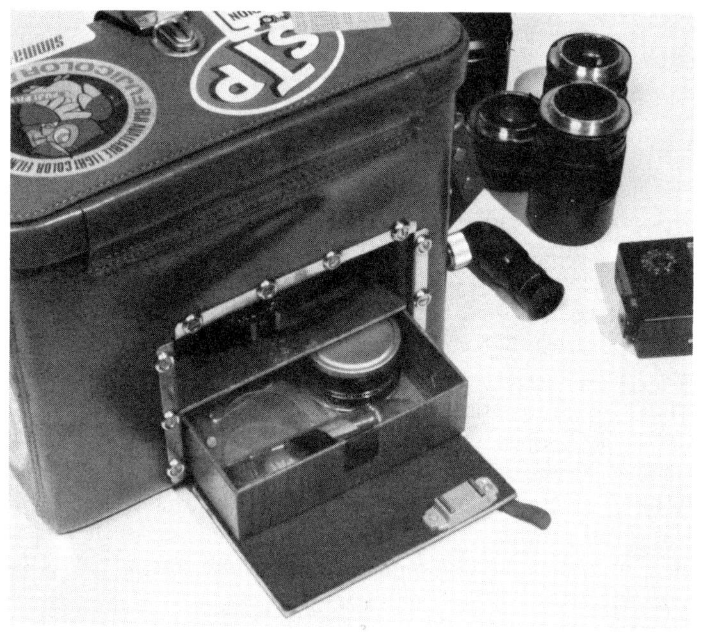

Small rear door with magnetic catch has been built to allow use of all space beneath the three short lenses above. Opening has shelf for second camera body and a drawer for kit of camera repair tools, filters, lens brush, and small tripod.

passport and wallet. And this is the smaller of the two bags shown in the photos.

The larger bag has room for four lenses: 24 mm, 50 mm, 135 mm and 300 mm. In addition, there is a larger film area for 14 rolls, room for a second camera body, kit of tools, small strobe, tripod, cable release, a larger selection of filters, waist-level finder for the Konica, and a drawer for even more little items.

In this larger bag, a small door was cut into the back of the bag to afford access to the large space beneath all lenses but the 300 mm. This is where the second camera body is to be carried and where the drawer is located for the extra equipment.

Both bags were carefully designed exactly as described above—from the inside out. Each works as intended. There are places for all lenses so that one can be put away before the next is selected. Film is readily available and can be changed quickly. Everything is easily accessible.

Checking Out Your Equipment

Before you take off on your trip, it is a pretty good idea to make a few simple precautionary checks on your camera and accessories.

If your camera uses batteries, be sure to start on your trip with fresh ones. They don't cost much and if you have old ones that expire while you're on your way, you might not even know it—until you see your finished pictures. Nicad batteries, which are used in cameras, have a rather long life, and read out fine right up to the end. Then, nothing—nothing, that is, but bad pictures.

Check out your shutter to be sure that all shutter speeds are at least functioning. While you are hardly expected to have a shutter speed timer in your home, you can at least open the camera back, remove the lens, and then click and wind through enough frames to see if the shutter is working. If all is not well, take the camera to a repair shop; when it is returned, shoot a roll of pictures and have them processed.

If your lenses are automatic, check each one to be sure the mechanical linkage at the rear of the lens is operating freely. Then put each lens on the camera and, with the back open, check to be sure that the lenses are stopping down as they should be during exposure. Try this at various shutter speeds. At the various shutter speeds, the lens should be stopping down to different apertures.

With a proper dusting brush, clean your camera and lenses inside and out for dust and grit. Be extremely careful not to touch any of the delicate parts inside the camera, such as the reflex mirror or the blades or curtains of your shutter. Then, with lens cleaning tissue or a soft lintless cloth, thoroughly clean both front and rear surfaces of your lenses. Dirty lenses make bad pictures.

Batteries in your little strobe light should also be checked. If they're penlights, you will be able to replace them nearly anywhere in the world. But to be sure, take a good supply with you. (Because these little batteries are so widely available, try to outfit yourself with as many travel items as possible that operate on them. Shaver, tape recorder, strobe, and radio all work on standard penlight batteries.) Long-life batteries are a good investment—especially for trips such as you're planning.

Camera First Aid

Because you can't always expect to find a first-class repair service, here are some first aid tips for your camera during your trip. Unless a truck runs over your camera, you can do some of the simpler repairs yourself.

If you own a 35 mm SLR camera, one of the most common and frustrating things that can happen is for the shutter to jam or lock. When this happens, you won't be able to trip the shutter or advance the film.

Remove the lens from your camera and lay it aside. With a toothpick or something small and delicate (not your finger), press up lightly on the mirror, while at the same time pressing down gently on the shutter release. This might free the mechanism right away. If not, try two other simultaneous applications of gentle pressure, for example on the shutter release and the auto diaphragm pin (located under the mirror) or on the mirror itself.

What has happened inside the camera body is that the intricate chain of events, which must occur in the right sequence, occasionally does not happen as it should. By ever so gently nudging these little parts from more than one direction at the same time, you can usually free things yourself. This is to be tried only when you are in real trouble and can't find a competent repair service.

If your automatic exposure system fails to work even though you have installed new batteries, it may be that you have a problem with the contacts where the battery is placed. By rubbing the contacts with a penknife, you can usually free the surface so that you will have a good connection.

If you should be unfortunate enough to drop your camera, look for a repairperson as soon as you can and have him or her check everything over. This is essential, for while the camera may have suffered no apparent damage, in fact the focus may be all out of adjustment. If no repair service is immediately available, at least shoot a quick roll of pictures and have them processed right away. The results will speak for themselves.

PRACTICE SHOOTING AT HOME

Once you have completed your camera kit and everything is packed and ready to go, get out in your home town and do a day's shooting—just as you plan to do on your trip. Call this a shakedown day if you like. You will be glad you did it. You may discover things you should be taking along and had forgotten or that something needs changing in your camera bag.

Try to treat your town as a new city that you have never seen before. Go after the best possible shots you can make with the widest possible variety of subjects.

If you will pretend that you are already on your trip abroad, you can cover your town with new eyes. You will begin to see features of the place which you never took the time to see. The best part of doing this trial run is that you'll be working the "bugs" out of your camera kit; you will also be assured that everything is working right and that your exposure and processing will be exactly as you want them to be.

While on this outing, consider the design of your camera bag insert. Is it comfortable? Or is there one last-minute change you might make to perfect it? Are your lenses readily accessible? Can you change film easily and quickly? Do you have enough film with you for a full day's shooting? What about the special filters—can you get at them without tearing your gadget bag apart? Is the shoulder strap comfortable—or should you add a little foam-rubber padding under that part which sits on your shoulder? Does your camera get caught on the shoulder strap of your gadget bag? If so, is there a way you can change it? Now is the time to do all these little things that will smooth things out for the trip.

In the evening, go over what you did and make notes. Take care of those little problems that came up while they're still fresh in your mind.

Mini-Portfolio

Those pictures which you have just shot of your home town may be used for making a little portfolio of pictures to take with you on your trip. When you travel, you will have pictures with you to show the new friends you make. They will be impressed that you even thought to bring along pictures of your own home town! There will be many situations where you can pass out your little packet of pictures—around the dinner table, on the airplane, in a pub. This will quickly open doors, and total strangers won't be strangers for long. You'll find that these people will be very interested in you.

Your portfolio should be pocket size, small enough to keep in one of those little nooks and crannies of your fitted-out camera bag. You might make them 3" × 5", the same size as your pocket notes. If you don't do your own darkroom work, have 3½" × 5" prints made commercially and trim a half-inch off one side.

Here is a brief list of subjects you can shoot in your home town that will interest people on your trip and that would make a fine mini-portfolio:

Local policeman in full uniform
Trash truck with crew
City Hall
Your family and family car
Inside and outside views of your home
Your family sitting at the dinner table
Inside and outside your place of worship
Local swimming-hole or beach with bathers
Drive-in movie theatre
Best and worst restaurants in town

Of course, you may add any other subjects you think would make your portfolio more interesting and would show your photographic talent off to best advantage. Remember, the people you meet on your trip are just as interested in seeing your town as you are in seeing theirs.

INSURANCE

Since you are going to be traveling all over the place, you should think about insuring your cameras and gear. The small price of protection might well be worth the money spent.

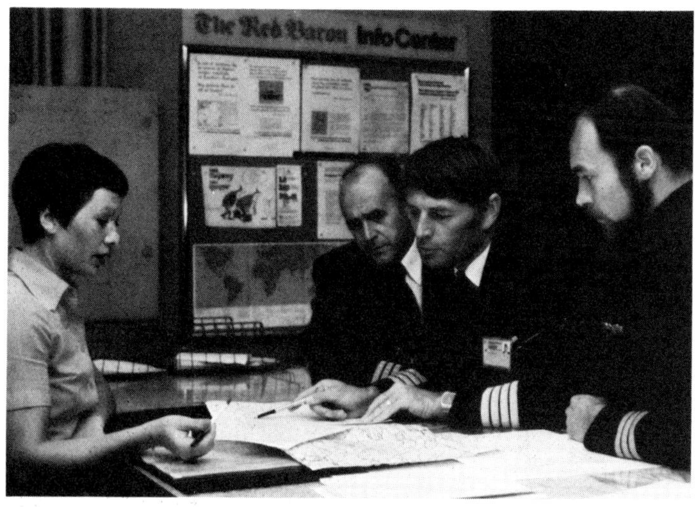

An operations employee gives pilot, co-pilot, and engineer final instructions and briefing for their flight. Pictures like this one add personal interest to your trip portfolio.

Some photographers rely upon their homeowners' insurance policies. Such a policy will usually cover cameras up to a maximum amount. However, there is usually a deductible clause, which means that you pay up to a certain amount of the replacement cost before the insurance company takes over. It would be a good idea to check with your agent to see if you are already protected in this way.

The agent will probably suggest that you buy a personal-articles "floater" policy. With such a policy you must list each item to be covered, along with serial numbers and other identifying marks. This is the most comprehensive protection. Remember, though, to inform your agent if and when you buy any new items, as you are only protected for those items in his file. The personal-articles floater can cover many objects besides photographic equipment. Such a policy is not expensive.

It is also possible to buy a short-term policy to cover all of your equipment for the duration of your planned trip. This is obviously less expensive than the year-round floater.

PICTURES ARE ONLY A PART OF YOUR TRIP

Keep your picture shooting in balance with the other aspects of your trip. In other words, shoot pictures of your trip, rather than build your trip around pictures. This is especially true if you are traveling with a companion. He or she must be considered first, as it is a trip for you both and not just for you and your camera. There will be plenty of time for you to take your pictures as well as to spend with your companion. Sometimes, you can split up for a morning or an afternoon so you can each do what you want. You both should go where you both want to go, and you can still make many truly good pictures without taking away from the enjoyment of the other.

3

Off You Go

LEAVING THE U.S.

Please don't think that U.S. Customs is only a coming home situation. Coming home, you will face such questions as what you have to declare, how much of whatever you are bringing into the country is duty-free, and how much you must pay according to where, why, and for how long you were away, and so forth.

Certificate of Registration

When you leave the United States, it is most important that you stop in at the U.S. Customs office at the airport or dock or border crossing. It is important that you have evidence before leaving home that any foreign-made items you are taking with you were actually purchased before your trip. Cameras, watches, and other easily identified imported items will be subject to close scrutiny as to place of purchase when you return home, and may have duties levied on them if there is any possibility that they were purchased on your trip. And remember, just because you were not in Japan does not prove you didn't purchase a Japanese-made camera in a tax-free shop elsewhere in the world.

To avoid any problems, all you need to do is stop in at U.S. Customs shortly before you check in for your overseas flight. Special Customs forms are available for you to fill out, listing all of your equipment down to the last roll of film, if you like. Then, when you have completed the simple form, a Customs inspector will probably ask you to show some or all of the items listed. You'd better have them available to show at this point. You have just listed what you are carrying with you and it should be there for inspection.

The Customs form is a 4" × 6" card called a Certificate of Registration. Space for listing all items which you should register is rather limited. Therefore, you may append to this a list detailing each item, along with serial numbers, model numbers, and other identification. If you are adding your own list, in the space on the form where you are to list each item merely write in, "see attached list."

If everything is in order, the Customs official will stamp the form and your list, staple them together, and you are set to go. In the accompanying illustration, we have reproduced an actual listing of photo gear and attached Certificate of Registration so you will see what to expect.

X-RAY AT AIRPORTS

A lot has been written about whether you should allow airport security people to x-ray your luggage. Our answer is yes and no. Yes, they may x-ray your suitcase but no, they may *not* x-ray your shoulder bag containing film or your camera bag—also containing film. The best information we are able to get on this subject of whether x-rays will affect your film is that it may—slightly. Each additional exposure adds a little bit more. At some undetermined point your film may have built up a fog layer that can create problems when you are trying to make optimum quality pictures.

To avoid exposing the film to x-rays, keep it with you in your camera bag and your shoulder bag. When you

Bob Mitchell!

January 12, 1979

United States Customs
Miami, Florida

Gentlemen;

I am traveling to Venezuela with the Purdue University Band as
their photographer and shall be taking the following photographic
equipment with me;

35mm Konica model T3 camera body (black) #662578

35mm Konica model T3 camera body (chrome) # 1215 of 1500

50mm f; 1.4 lens for above #7604722

135mm f: 3.2 lens for above #3382596

24mm f: 2.8 lens for above # 6632591

300mm f: 4.5 lens for above # 6952032

Rollei model 121BC strobe light for above

Sincerely

Robert W. Mitchell

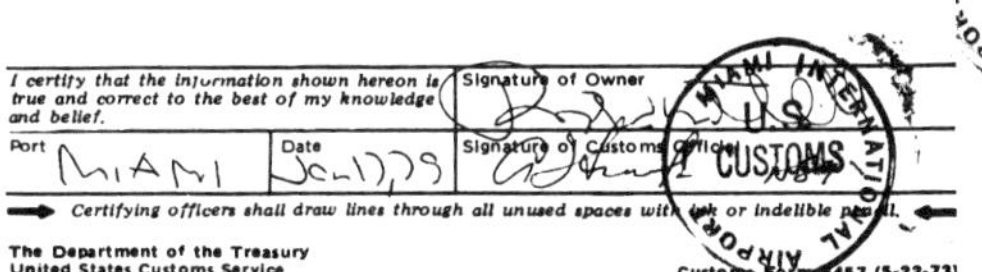

35

go through the security check, ask the security people (who are employed by the airline) to *please* hand inspect your hand baggage because it contains photographic film. Usually they are quite cooperative, but don't let them push you around on this point. They may point to an official-looking sign which says that their equipment will not affect your film and then try to take your hand baggage from you to pass it onto the conveyor belt. Be polite but firm. If necessary, take down the inspector's name and ask to see his or her supervisor. Find the supervisor and again, ask if you can't *please* have your hand baggage hand inspected. If you still have problems, ask for the airline station manager. *He* will help you, rest assured. After all, you're not asking for the sky—just a little personal attention.

FOREIGN CUSTOMS

Depending upon the country you are entering, you may expect incoming tourists to be treated with anything from total indifference to a complete inspection of baggage and person. In certain parts of the world, customs officials are (often justifiably) nervous about possible security threats; other nations are extremely vigilant about drug trafficking. Should you happen to be subjected to an extremely thorough search, remain cool and don't attempt to avoid it. Presumably you have nothing to hide, and the worst that can happen is you'll have to repack your entire gear on the floor in the middle of a busy terminal. Chalk it up to experience.

A special Customs note: Always assume that the Customs person with whom you are dealing has absolutely no sense of humor. Don't act smart. A misunderstood joke can cause more trouble than it's worth.

IMMIGRATION

Upon your arrival in a new country, Immigration people will want to see your passport. A couple of questions concerning the purpose of your visit (tourist) and the length of your stay usually suffice. If they ask you if you're a professional photographer, by all means tell them no. Otherwise, you will find yourself in competition with the local photographers and may need a special permit to work in the country. Just tell them you're a tourist—even if you *do* have a black camera and the clerk in the camera shop told you that it was a professional model. A black camera does not a professional make.

FIRST DAY'S SHOOTING

When you arrive at a new location, start shooting pictures as soon as possible and keep it up while everything is totally foreign to you. This sounds strange, but it makes sense. Before even a couple of days have passed, the newness of your environment will wear off and you'll become used to what you are seeing. The initial excitement of what you see in a city is what you want to capture in your pictures.

Look for features of this new place that you think are really unusual, that stand out. It may be the architecture, or the people's faces, or the children, or possibly the way people dress. Save yourself a lot of editing time back home by trying to determine what is real picture material before you waste miles of film on something you could have shot in your own country. This is a good point to keep in mind whenever you're shooting in a foreign country: Is this really different or could it have been shot back home? There probably aren't all that many donkey carts on your block back home—so if one passes by, go ahead and take a chance. It might be a winner.

NOTES

Don't forget to take along a supply of blank 3" × 5" cards to write down details of things you will want to remember. Don't try to write down everything that happens or everything you do on the whole trip, or you'll find yourself doing nothing else. But a few simple notes will be useful when you return home.

You may want to remember what exposure you used in that darkest of all cathedrals in southern Germany. Was it a second at f/5.6? If so, you may want to know later. But there is no reason in the world to write down every exposure you make. You know what you did and how you did it. Did Rembrandt write down what number brush he used on such and such a painting? Of course not!

Places or names are not easy to remember. These are notes you should try to keep. That fellow who helped you out when you needed to get to the airport in Rome in a hurry to make an early flight should receive a thank-you letter after you have returned home. Or where was that great bar you found in northern Spain? Write it down.

So, don't forget to take a supply of blank 3″ × 5″ cards along with all those fresh batteries and all that film.

4

How to Shoot Travel Pictures

EXPOSURE CONTROL

None of your pictures are going to be worth much to you or anyone else if they aren't carefully exposed. There is no excuse for anything less these days—what with the excellent cameras with built-in exposure meters and the fine hand-held meters for non-automatic cameras. You should be working on this part of your photography long before your trip so that you can be assured of first quality negatives or slides every time. Remember—no excuses. Find a way of doing it right always. Make proper exposure a habit.

Assume that each picture you shoot will be the really big one of the trip. Check and double check your exposure when you have time, and try to be ready to shoot at all times should something happen in front of you that calls for immediate action.

Learn all you can about the mechanics of picture shooting during the planning stage of your trip. When you're over there shooting, it's already too late. Your camera, by then, should be a part of you.

SUBJECT INTEREST

How many times have you been forced to look at just plain boring travel pictures? Have you wondered why this happens? For one thing, those pictures probably lacked interest; they may have been only a collection of postcard-type views. Pictures and views are not the same thing. Take one of those postcard views and add a story-telling figure or group of people and you then have a picture.

In fact, it would be a good idea for you to buy post-cards in each city you visit. Study these cards to see where the photographer was situated when he made the pictures. Then try to determine how you would shoot the same pictures and how you would make them more lifelike. With a little practice, you can begin to create truly inter-esting pictures—ones you will enjoy for a long time to come, and ones over which your friends will exclaim rather than yawn. It's not easy to rave when you're yawn-ing!

When you have positioned yourself exactly where the postcard photographer did, calculate your exposure and get set to shoot. Now wait. And wait some more. Wait for some little old lady to walk into the scene, adding some human interest. Then shoot. Get a couple of shots off if possible, making sure to have at least one good one.

Don't immediately move on for another shot. Sit like a duck hunter, waiting for something even better to happen on your little stage. Look! Here comes an old man holding hands with his little grandson. Just when he gets to stage right, he tips his hat to the local priest. Things are looking better! Click that shutter before the whole thing dissolves before your eyes. They won't run it through again for you. If fact, if you are seen, the whole mood will be lost. Try to look like you're waiting for a streetcar or something. Bring your camera up to your eye only at the last minute—with just time enough to compose and shoot. Your shutter speed, aperture, and focus should already be set; you are now working with what is only a simple box camera. Point and shoot; the result should be most satis-factory.

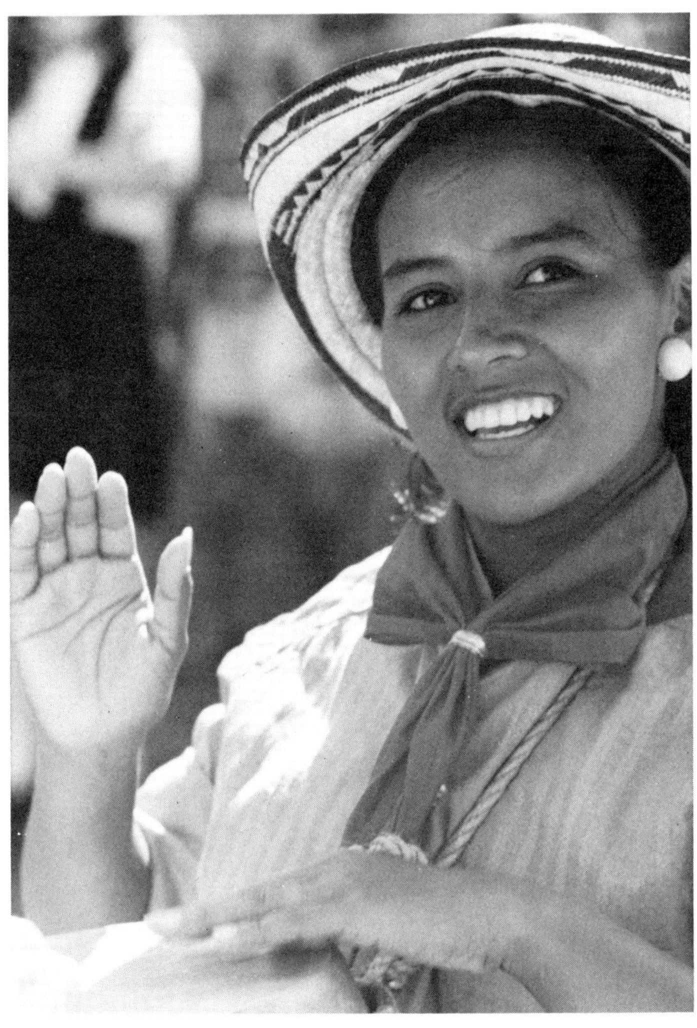

The radiant smile and poised hands of this Colombian folk musician tell it all. The bongo she is playing isn't even in the picture, but you know instantly what she is doing. This backlighted picture required no special exposure adjustment since most of the scene was in shadow. Distraction of a somewhat cluttered background is avoided by keeping it out of focus. Taken with a 50 mm lens; 1/500 sec. at f/5.6.

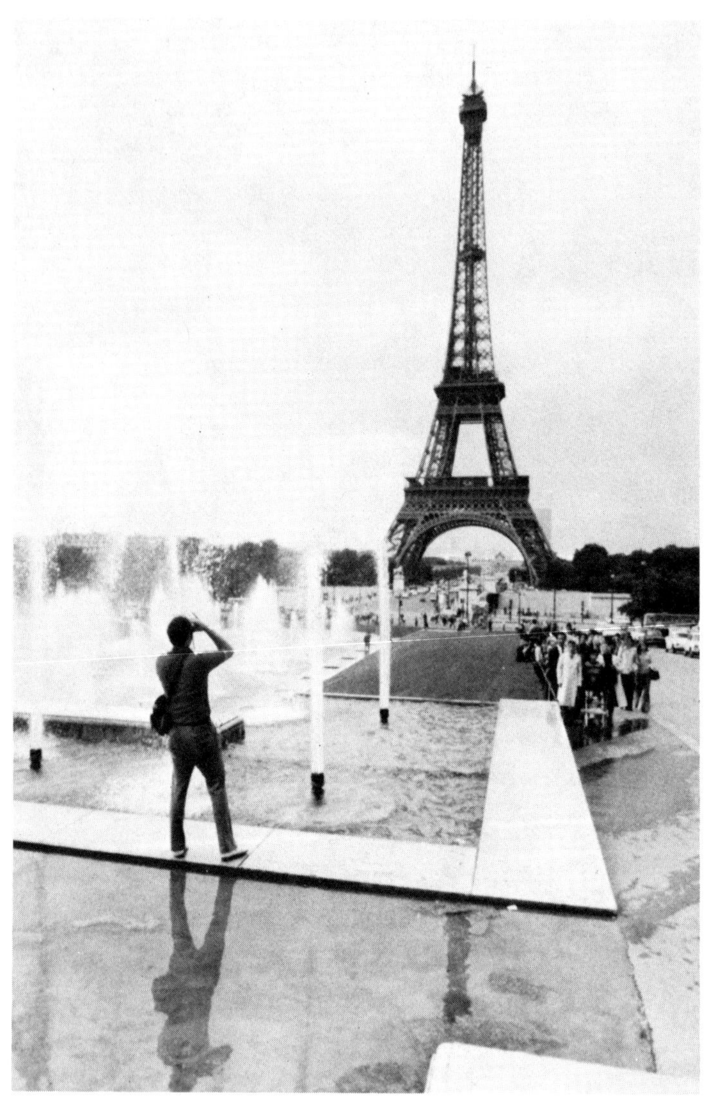

A 24 mm lens was used to take in the full height of this really tall landmark. Everything was going for this picture: the tower, fountains, clouds, and re-flections. Exposure was 1/250 sec. at f/8.

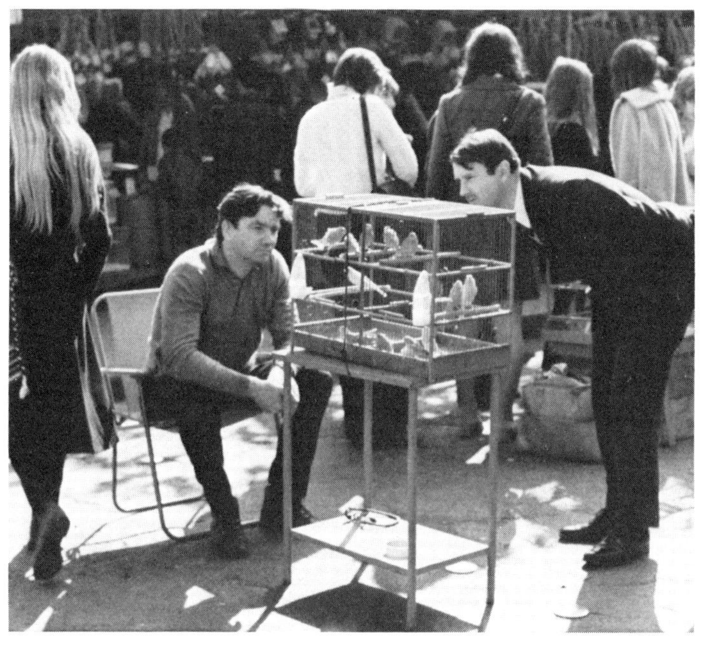

*Birds in cages are rather uninteresting. But if you find cages such
as these in the Paris bird market on a Sunday morning—along
with the seller, a possible buyer, and a young woman passing by—
you have a picture worth shooting. This was taken with a
50 mm lens; 1/250 sec. at f/16.*

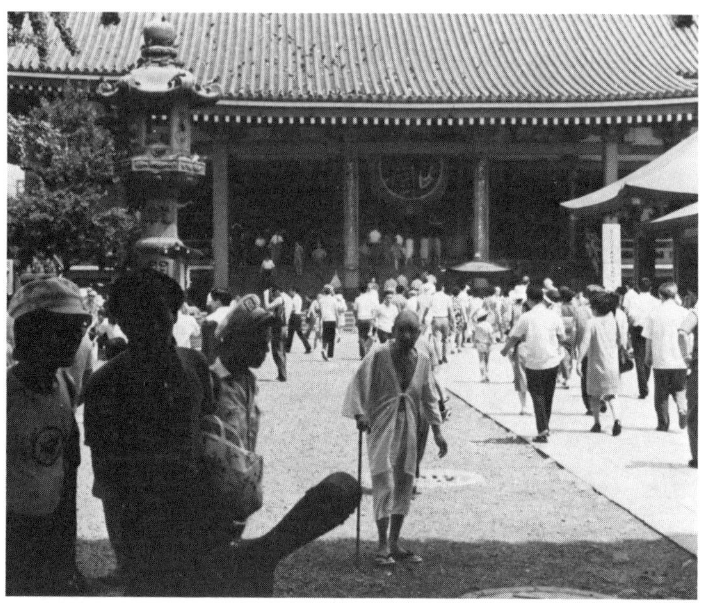

This scene was taken in a temple in the heart of Tokyo. Note the very large lantern hanging near the entrance, and the contrast between the guitar-carrying youth and the venerable old gentleman. Taken with a 50 mm lens; 1/250 sec. at f/5.6.

The question to ask yourself is "What does this shot need that will make it a really terrific picture?" Once you understand this, your pictures will be much more successful.

ARC SHOOTING

This is one way of photographing people without their ever knowing it. Let's say you're standing ten feet from a person who you simply *must* photograph, but you don't want to make him or her camera-conscious. Should you tip your hand and point your camera at your subject, the candid effect would be lost.

Look anywhere but directly at this person while you're planning your composition. Find an object or a point to his or her left or right but the same distance away from you. Aim your camera at this object and focus carefully. This assures that you are also focused on your subject, but even though he may be looking right at you, he is still unaware that he is about to be photographed. Assuming you have already adjusted your camera for exposure, you are now ready to shoot.

Aiming at that focusing point, with your camera up to your eye, slowly move the camera in an arc so that you move toward your subject. As he appears in your finder at the ideal instant, trip your shutter but continue to move through this arc until you have passed him. Now lower your camera and look long and carefully at the last point of your arc at which your camera was pointing. *Never* look at your subject. He can be looking directly at you, but unless he is a photographer, he will never know that you have just taken his picture. It works! It's called never making eye contact. In fact, your subject will probably turn around and try to figure what in the world you were photographing over in that direction.

Try to collect a wide variety of portraits—not all of old people, not all beautiful people, and not all young children. Get a mixed bag of what you see and your finished selection of pictures will be a true cross-section of life as you saw it on your trip.

COMPOSITION

Composition in a picture is merely the pleasing arrangement of the various elements of the scene as you position them in your frame. You may think you can't change what's before you, but you can. By framing, isolating, featuring, you can make the scene appear just the way you want it. You can change from one lens to another to frame your picture the way you like. Don't become lazy, though. Rather than making a lens change, you may be able to achieve the same result by walking a few feet toward or away from your subject.

Composition is not a subject that is easily taught. There are some vague rules of composition that speak of S-curves and placement of the main center of interest. But when all is said and done, it is the initial arrangement of the elements of the picture that *you* must like before it is to be judged as good or bad composition.

The best way to learn composition is to see what others are doing and have done in the past. Painters—the Old Masters—were just that: masters—of composition. Study some of their paintings; they demonstrate a superb sense of what goes where and how much of each element of the picture should be shown.

Another place to study composition is at the movies and on television. Film and video cameramen are masters of their art, and just watching what they are doing is worthwhile. The subject is immaterial—daytime soap operas, sports events, travel shows—all teach how a fixed horizontal format can be utilized to show any scene off to best advantage. Even a golf match can display this mastery of composition. Consider that these cameramen are working "live," constantly changing scene, zeroing in close or moving back for a long shot before your eyes.

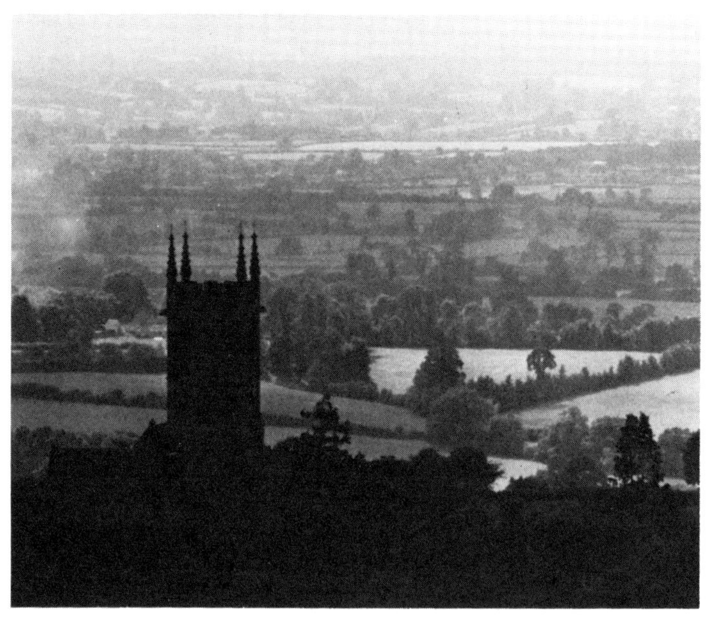

This is the English countryside at its best. Stand on a hill in Shaftesbury, Dorsetshire, and, looking off into the Vale of Blackmore, this is what you see. The haze in the distance makes it especially lovely, with the village in shadow. Taken with a 135 mm lens; 1/125 sec. at f/11.

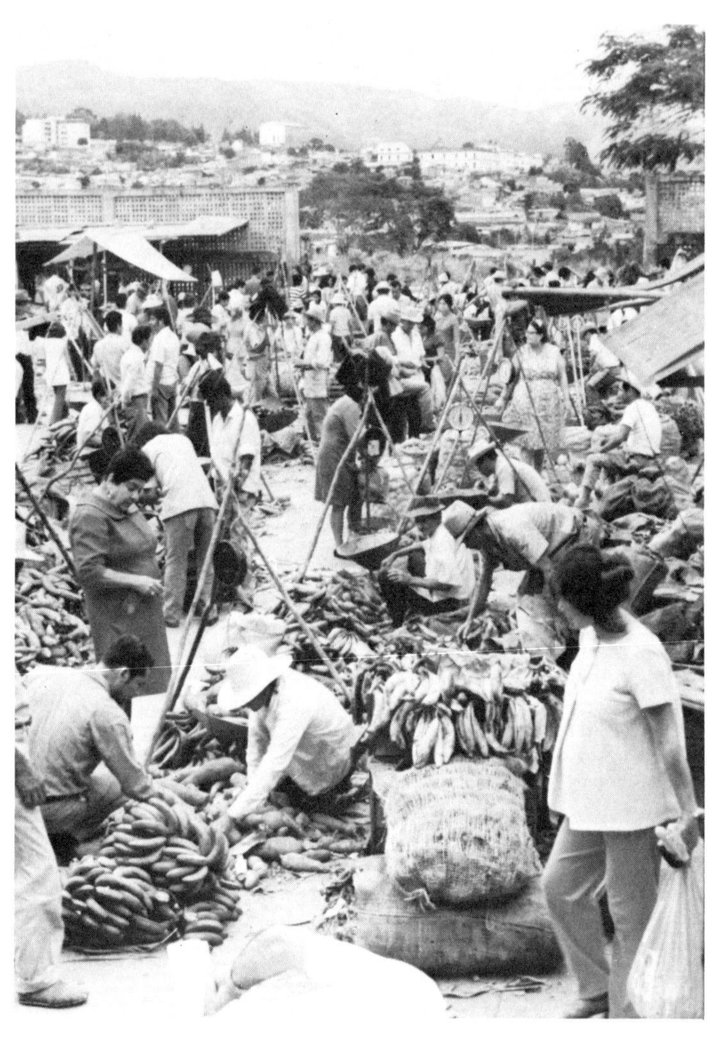

One would think an art director had set up this scene—it is too perfect to have simply happened. This is the city market in San Cristobal, high up in the Andes in Venezuela. Each person is in exactly the right place, and the background is exactly right, too. Taken with a 50 mm lens; 1/250 sec. at f/11.

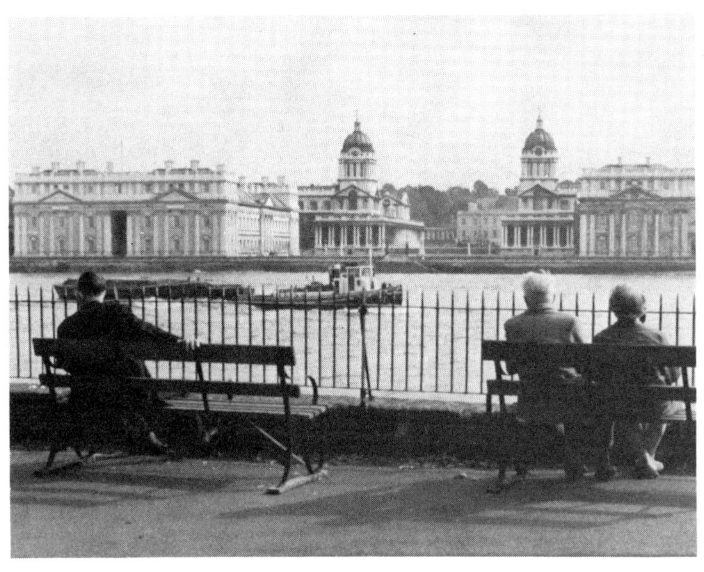

View from across the River Thames of the Royal Naval College at Greenwich, designed by Sir Christopher Wren. By backing away slightly from the scene, the photographer was able to include the people on the park bench, thereby framing the scene for added interest. Taken with a 24 mm lens; 1/250 sec. at f/5.6.

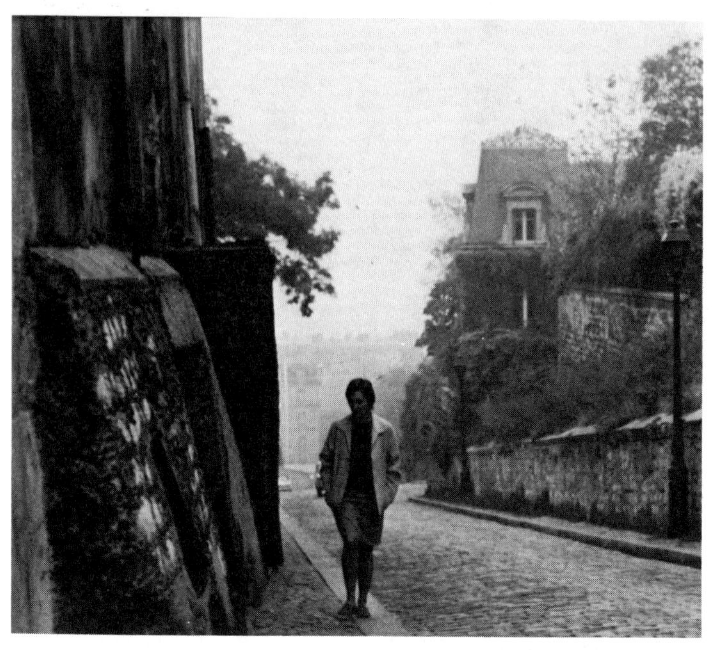

This photo of a street descending from Montmartre in Paris was made with a 50 mm lens and a medium shutter speed—1/250 sec. at f/8. Composition might be improved by reversing the negative, thereby allowing the eye to move from left to right as it scans the picture.

Top-notch newspaper photographers work the same way. What they do under pressure—at a fire, for example—is extraordinary. One photographer will back off and shoot through a burning doorway, the blackened embers forming a natural frame for some part of the building that is billowing smoke and flames. This is the sort of shooting you must teach yourself to do. You have a deadline too. Yours is the end of your trip and it's just as final and fixed as the putting to bed of the evening newspaper or the TV late news.

Many of your picture situations will unfold within the shortest possible time. You must be ready and make your move at exactly the right time—and your composition must be just right.

PERSPECTIVE CONTROL

When you aim your camera and tilt it upward or downward, the vertical lines no longer remain parallel but appear to converge at the top and bottom of the picture respectively. This is most evident when you photograph buildings and especially when you use a wide-angle lens.

Professional photographers who use studio cameras or view cameras are able to correct for this vertical distortion by tilting the actual film plane so that it is absolutely straight up and down, and by tilting the board upon which the camera lens is mounted. Unfortunately, this can't be done with a twin-lens or SLR. While there are lenses called P.C. (perspective correction) lenses—they don't really do what you want.

The three accompanying pictures of the Doges' Palace in Venice illustrate the situation. The first picture shows what you can expect if you tilt your camera with wide-angle lens upward. The vertical lines in the scene appear to converge toward the top of the picture.

Seek out a point in the scene which is at the same elevation as your camera lens and place that point in the

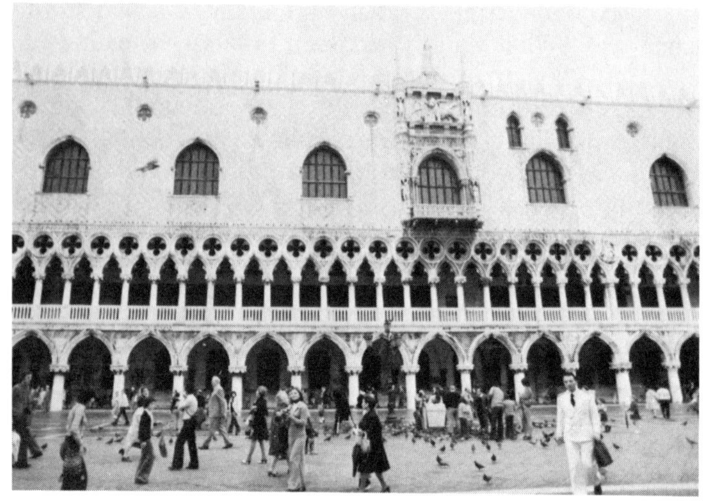

When the camera is tilted upward to get all of the height of a building in the picture, the vertical lines appear to converge at the top. This and the other two shots in this series were taken with a 24 mm lens; 1/250 sec. at f/11.

center of your viewfinder or on a line parallel to the center of your viewfinder. In doing this, you will have automatically made the back of your camera exactly vertical, thereby assuring that all vertical lines in the picture be parallel, as shown in the second picture of the series.

The problem now is that you don't have the top of the building in the picture any more, and you have rather more foreground than you would like. This is where the P.C. lenses are useful. They actually can be moved upward in their mounts so that the image projected onto the film is higher up. You can do the same thing by turning your camera for a vertical format. Again, square the back by

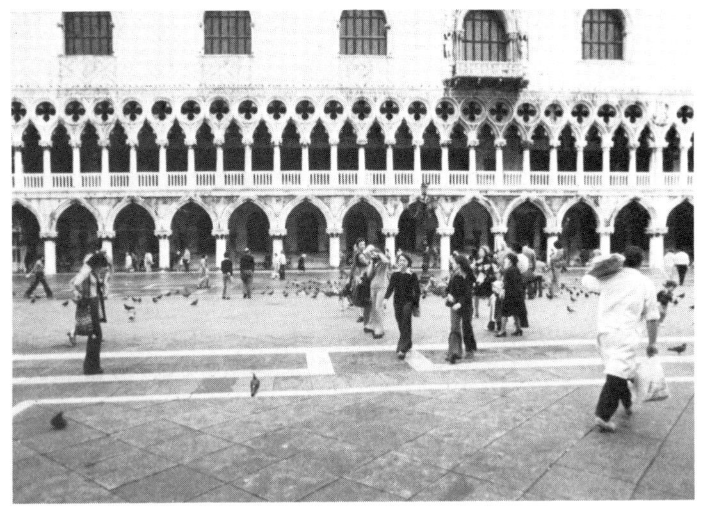

The same building as shown opposite can be corrected for vertical distortion if the back of the camera is made parallel to the subject. This can be done easily if the spot in the center of the viewfinder is made to fall on a line that is the same elevation as the lens. In order to keep the top of the building in the picture, move farther from the building, still keeping the camera parallel to it.

selecting that point in the scene which is at the same elevation as the lens, and place it level with the center of the viewfinder. As the third picture shows, the result is a much higher view of the building.

When you get into the darkroom, you can crop out the bottom area of the picture. The resulting picture will be very effective and you will have corrected for the vertical distortion. Many of the pictures in this book were shot with this scheme in mind. Note the interior of the Cologne Cathedral (see color section). Those verticals were achieved with a wide-angle lens. Some cropping was done in the darkroom to achieve this finished picture.

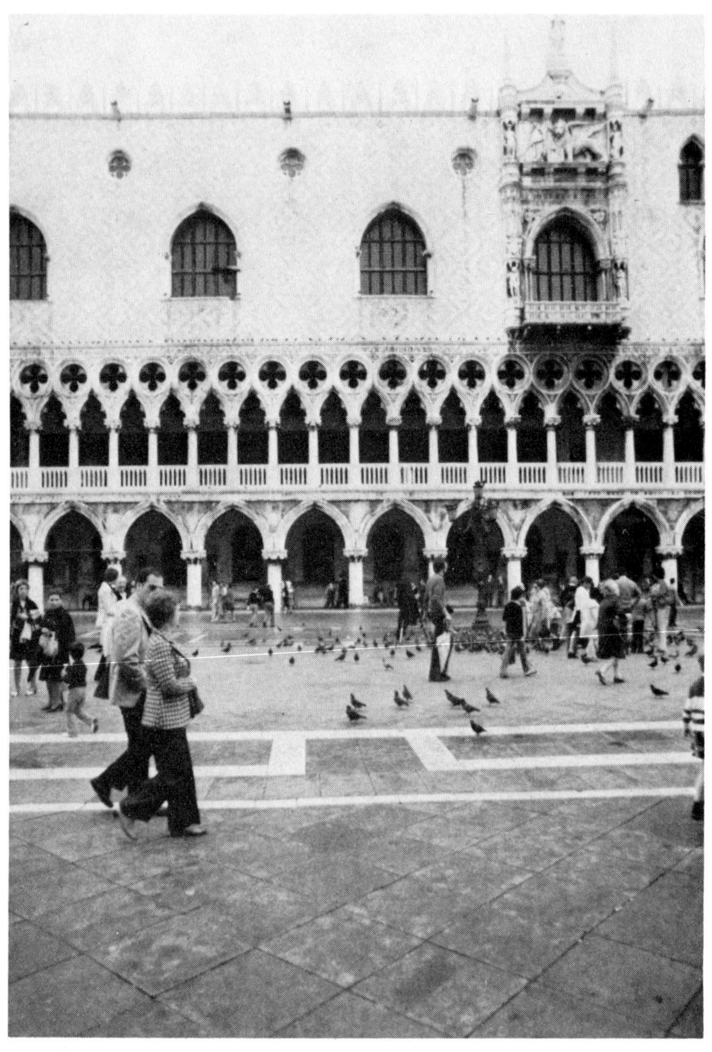

The same scene as on pages 52 and 53 can be improved if the camera is turned to the vertical format. Now, if the camera back is kept straight, it is possible to show the top of the building and keep the vertical lines correct.

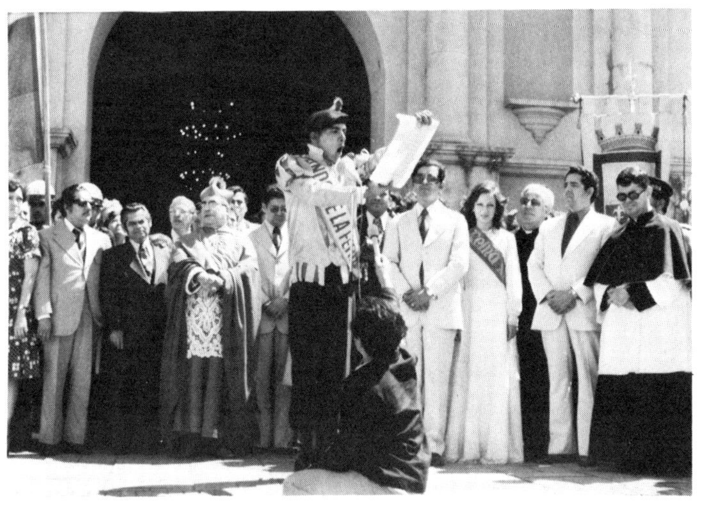

*Were this member of a presidential honor guard
not reading a proclamation, the large group of
people would make a rather dull photograph. As
it turns out, all the people in the picture are turned
to him and absorbed in what he is doing. The
photographer waited for him to open his mouth
fully to give a little extra impact to the occasion.
Taken with a 50 mm lens; 1/500 sec. at f/16.*

NEXT DAY'S PLAN

Each night, get out your notes and read carefully
those about the city you are now seeing. How do you stand
in terms of things you had planned to do? Is there enough
time left in your remaining days to accomplish what you
had hoped? If not, you had better weigh those remaining
items on your list, schedule the most important ones, and
scratch the others. Rather than fret over what you won't

have time to do, just be glad that you had the foresight to plan so completely that you are not sitting around wondering where to go next.

By looking over what remains to be done, and keeping in mind the weather forecast for the next day, you can begin to outline where you will go the next morning and what you will do. You can also plan where you will be at lunchtime; possibly a local acquaintance can suggest a good place to eat. The afternoon can also be outlined, and there you have your tentative day planned.

The next day should go according to plan unless you hear a marching band in the distance—signaling some sort of festival about which you were not informed. This is a time to change plans at once! There are so many unannounced festivals that a firm schedule is difficult to follow. Just remember that you are on holiday and you should do what you *want* to do—rather than what you think you *have* to do.

ATTITUDE

Early on in this book, we mentioned that we would be talking more about your attitude toward picture shooting on your trip. This can be your strongest suit if you can develop a good outlook on what you are doing with your camera.

Regardless of what happens to you—whether it is the weather, some official who tries to limit your picture taking, the fact that you must do a lot more walking or climbing in order to get a particular shot—each of these reasons, and many others, can turn you sour on further picture shooting, unless you have made up your mind that none of that sort of thing is going to spoil your fun. There's always a way around every problem you will encounter and you must learn the knack of only worrying about those things that are worth worrying about. Forget the others.

5

What to Shoot on Your Trip

Let's get down to considering those subjects that make ideal travel pictures. You needn't go out looking for these specific subjects. Just have them in mind as you move around and they will appear from time to time. Later, you can edit your total picture output down to only a few of each category. With this selected assortment of shots, you will have a terrific collection of pictures. Your work will have the touch of a true professional.

PEOPLE

Nothing should top this subject on your long list of what to photograph on your trip. More than any other aspect of the places you visit, people will reflect the spirit, character, and mood of what you are seeing.

Most people are willing to be included in your pictures if you treat them with proper courtesy and respect. Even if you can't speak their language, you can get across to them that you would like them to pose for you. Even better than posing them, try to include the locals in your pictures in a way that is completely relaxed and natu-ral. If you see a taxi driver polishing his 1952 taxi, it is obvious that he is really proud of his car. Photograph him at his work and then approach him for a portrait. Chances

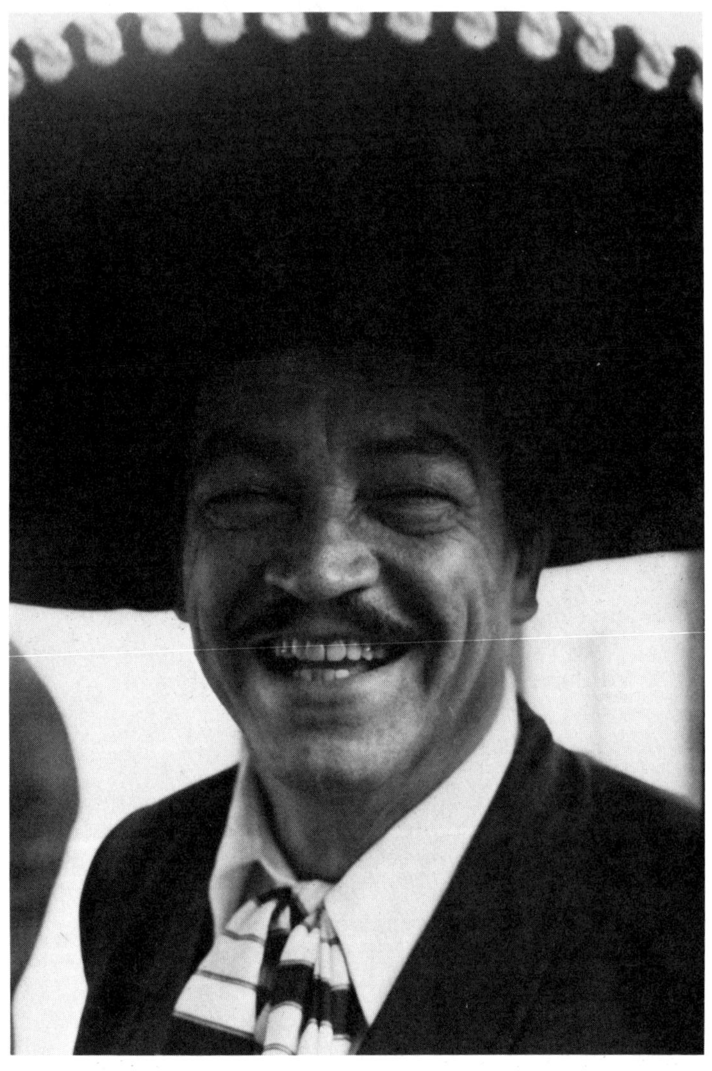

This member of a Mexican mariachi band was photographed with a 135 mm lens. The exposure was carefully metered for the shadow area of his face, with the background totally overexposed. Taken at 1/125 sec. at the lens's largest aperture—in this case, f/3.2.

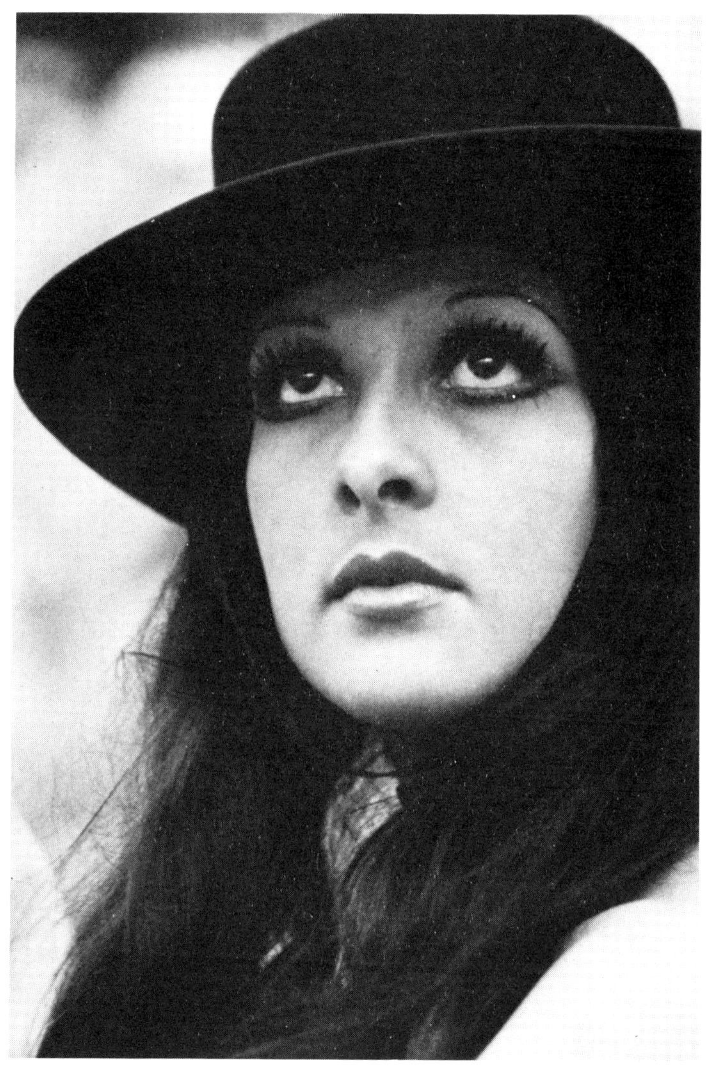

This beauty festival queen of the state of Tachira, Venezuela, was photographed at the Festival of San Sebastian. With a little direction through hand signs, several usable portraits were made with a 135 mm lens. This was taken at 1/500 sec. at f/5.6.

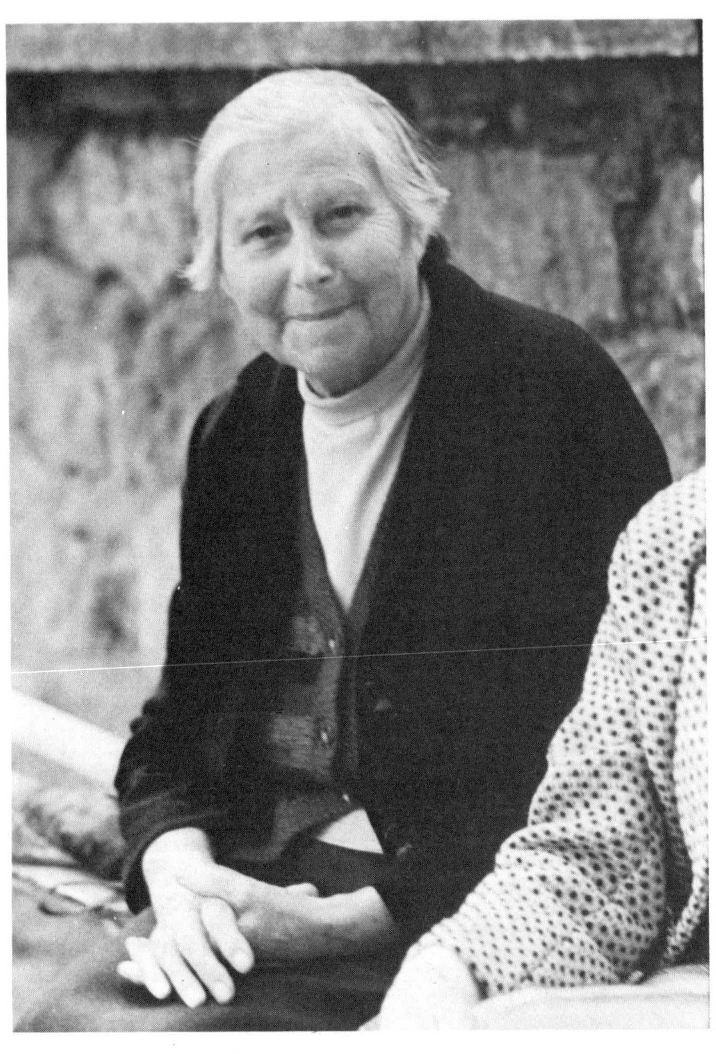

*The face of this handsome woman photo-
graphed in Montmartre is reminiscent of
certain of the paintings of the Flemish
masters. Taken with a 135 mm lens;
1/125 sec. at f/4.*

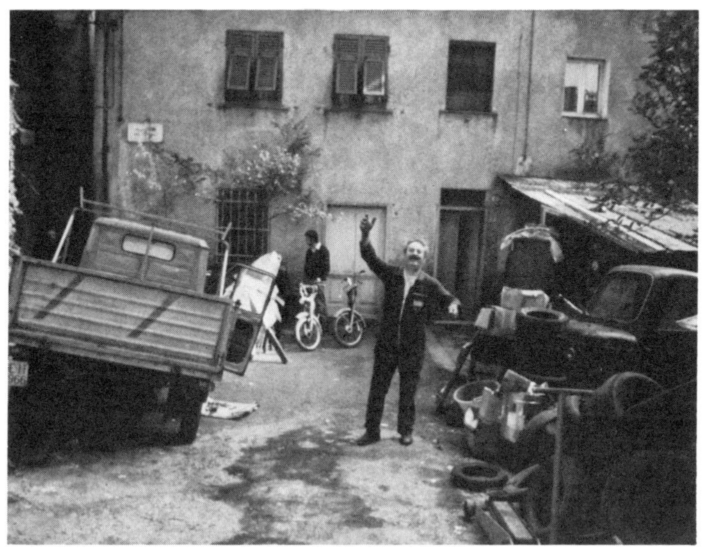

*This outgoing gentleman in Italy wanted to
pose in his outdoor automobile workshop. He
literally called out for attention. Taken with a
50 mm lens; 1/250 sec. at f/11.*

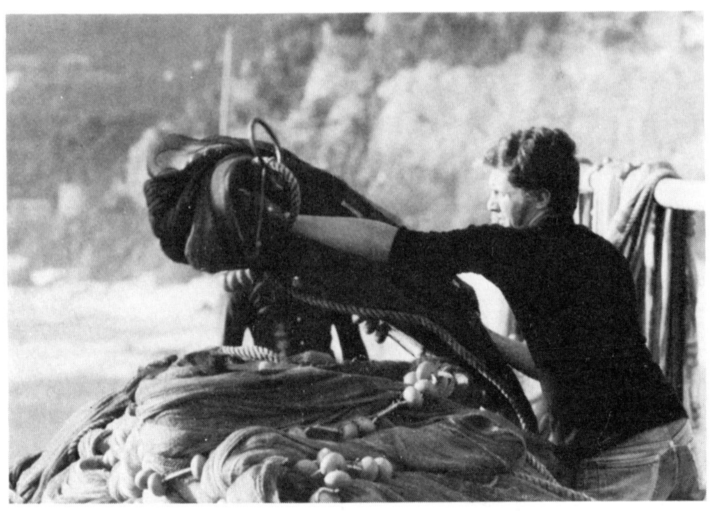

Here is a good example of how to depict motion in a still picture. This fisherman in Comalgi, Italy, is stacking newly repaired nets. By catching the action at the exact peak, the photographer has made a very lifelike still picture. Taken with a 135 mm lens; 1/1000 sec. at f/8.

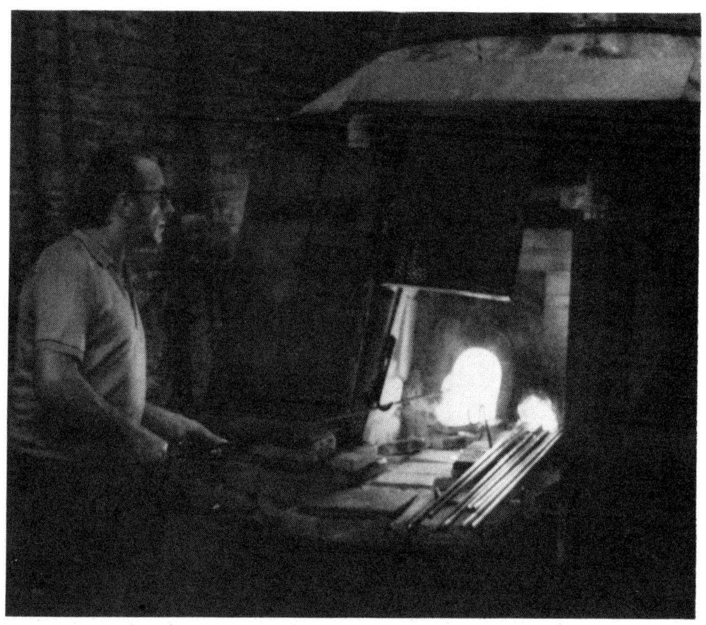

*A glass blower in one of Venice's world-famous factories
pulls molten glass from his oven. The subject was illum-
inated only by the light from the furnace and a small sky-
light above. This hand-held shot was taken with a 50 mm
lens at 1/15 sec. at f/4. Several exposures were made
for insurance; only this one was free of camera movement.*

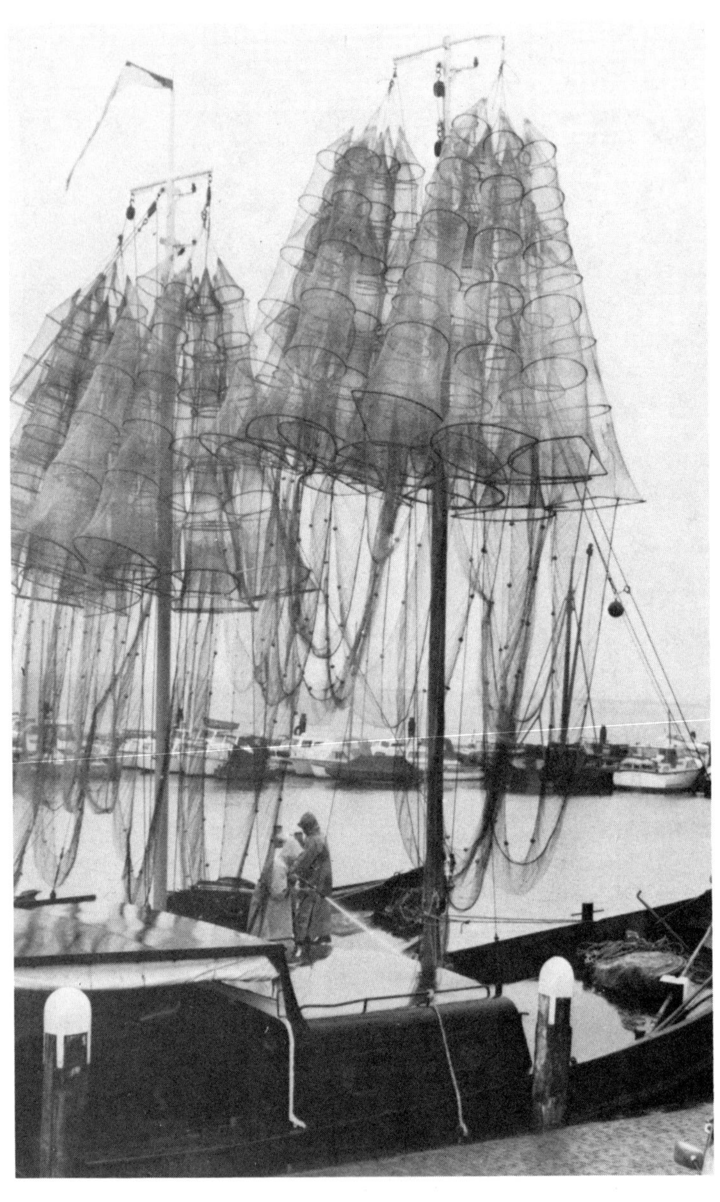

Eel nets drying in Volendam, Holland. The unusual and eye-catching pattern, with human figures for scale, make this an excellent composition. Taken with a 24 mm lens; 1/125 sec. at f/5.6.

Pearl divers in Toba, Japan, have just returned from a day's work. Close-ups of these young girls will also be worth shooting. Taken with a 135 mm lens; 1/500 sec. at f/11.

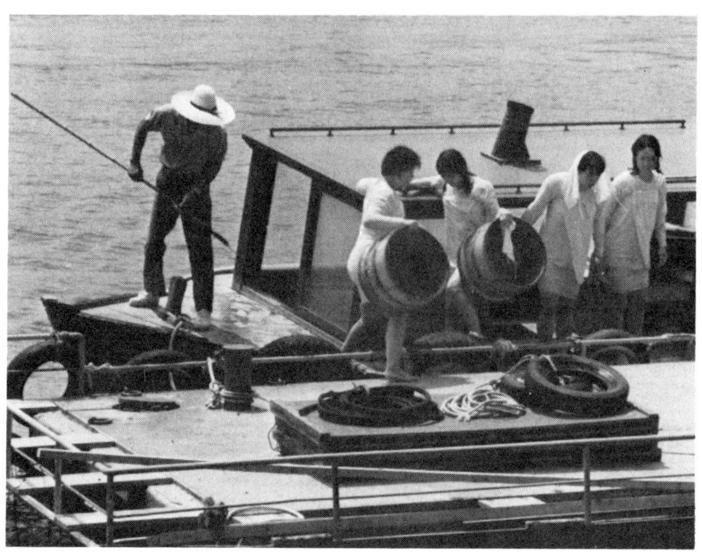

are that he will tighten up and the candid shot will be the best one. If not, you have both. If he freezes up for the portrait, you already have the best shot anyway.

When seeking out people to photograph, be sure to find those who really reflect the customs and dress of the country they represent. Dutch fishermen are a good illustration of this consideration. Those wonderful baggy pants they really wear on fishing boats are just what you and your camera have been seeking. If they are fixing a net or hauling a crate of fish into the local market, so much the better. In Belgium, lacemakers are certainly ideal portrait subjects. Closeup shots here could show details of the lace and the time-weathered faces and hands at work.

Children

Children anywhere in the world are superb picture subjects. They are entirely natural, so many of their activities make great pictures. On your trip, just keep an eye out for unusual child pictures and you'll come home with some show stoppers.

If you see a schoolteacher taking her class on a walking tour of the area, you'll see some good subjects for your camera. Children never seem to see cameras. If they do, they never let on that they know you're there.

Use a short telephoto lens and you'll be right on target without bothering them at all. Those little faces will give you a tremendous variety of expressions. In Paris, go to the outdoor puppet shows in the parks, and photograph the excited faces.

With luck, you will encounter a group of children playing street games of their country. They all have endless imagination and your pictures should show this in some way.

Any mother in the world would be proud to have you ask if you might photograph her little one. Do it. You'll be glad you did. Language should be no problem. All you need are a couple of hand signals.

Children watching a parade in a small mountain town in South America. Each child has a slightly different expression on his or her face. Taken with a 50 mm lens; 1/250 sec. at f/8.

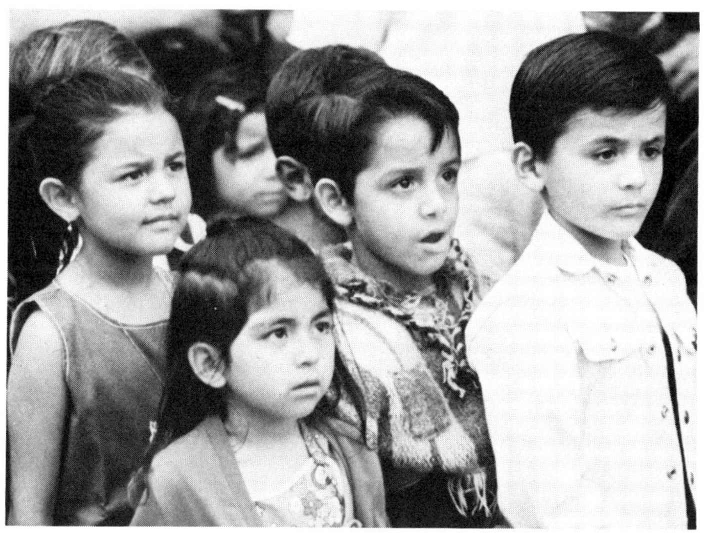

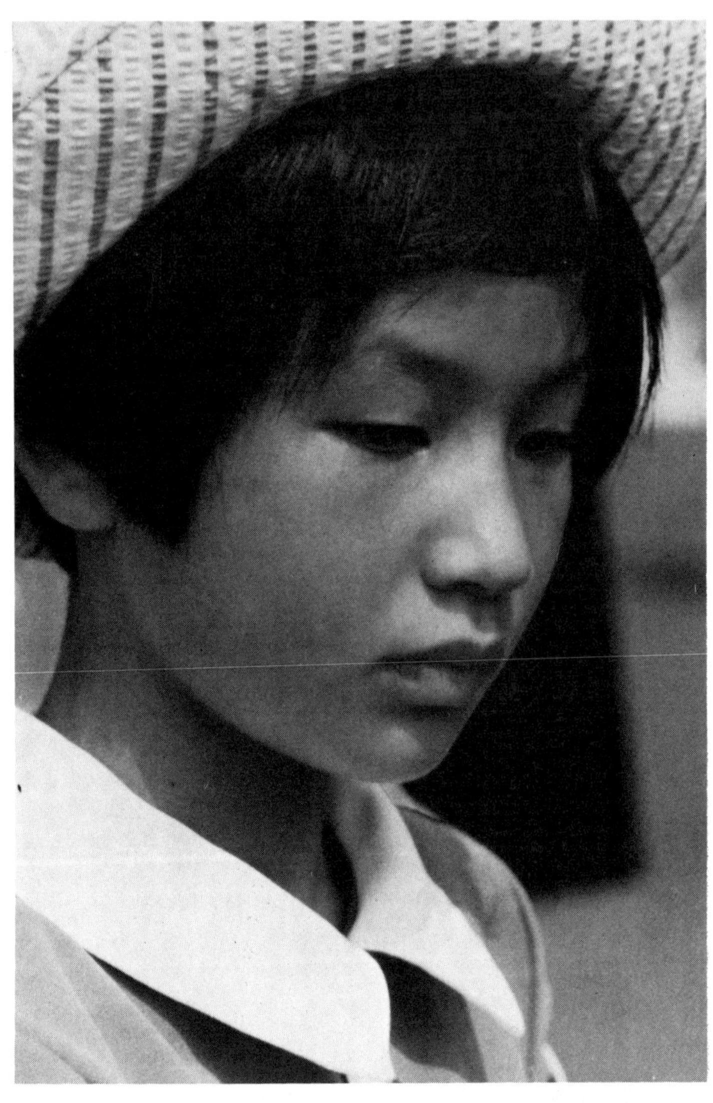

*This exquisite young schoolgirl in Tokyo
was entirely unaware of the camera,
as the short telephoto (135 mm) lens was
being used. Taken at 1/250 sec. at f/16.*

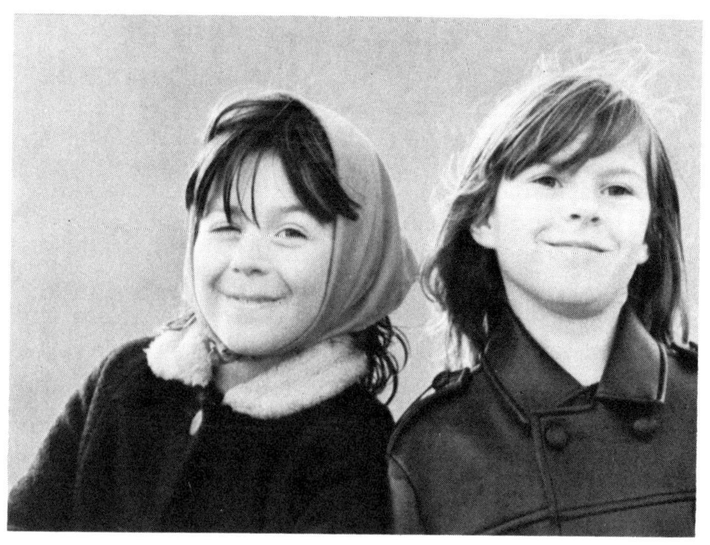

These two urchins in Plymouth, England, asked the photographer to take their picture. When he agreed, they demanded: "Give us sixpence to get 'ome." He did, only to then hear them say: "Each!" They knew what they were doing—but the photographer got the picture—out of Dickens. Note the very simple background selected for the shot. Taken with a 135 mm lens; 1/125 sec. at f/5.6.

Humor

Think back: How many really funny pictures have you made? It's not easy. Knowing this, you should still be on the lookout for some funny shots on your trip. How is it done? Who knows. One photographer was resting on a park bench after a full day's shooting all over London. Suddenly, he heard a noise a few yards over to the left, and there was an unmarked police car. Four rather sizable uniformed police jumped out of the car and immediately gave chase to a hippie-type house robber who had been down an areaway in front of a house. The chase started at stage left and proceeded to move directly across the photographer's field of view. Just as they reached stage right, the cops caught the robber! The photographer caught the whole episode on film. As luck would have it, the right lens (135 mm) was on the camera, and the camera was set for the right exposure. The resulting series of pictures are much like a comic strip sequence: 1) crook hears cops; 2) crook runs; 3) cops chase crook; 4) cops catch crook; 5) crook is led away in the arms of the law. Moral: Have your camera ready at all times because you never know what kind of picture situation will come up when you least expect it.

One picture almost got away. A policeman was writing a traffic ticket and the young lady in the car suddenly gave forth with the biggest yawn in the world. Nerves, no doubt.

Graffiti chalked on a wall in Oxford, England: "Writing on walls is the first sign of genius."

Washing hung out to dry on a Dutch barge in a stiff breeze: Three pairs of coveralls filled with the wind looked like three men helping the laundress hang themselves on the line!

An airborne matador—not by choice: It may not be funny to him but it does tickle the funnybone.

In Venezuela, a woman eating soup stares at her spoon, which has suddenly come up with a chicken claw in it. Is this a special delicacy, or some sort of joke?

A London bobby chases a burglar. As described in the text, the robber was duly caught and hauled off to court. Taken with a 135 mm lens; the camera was preset for any eventuality— 1/250 sec. at f/5.6.

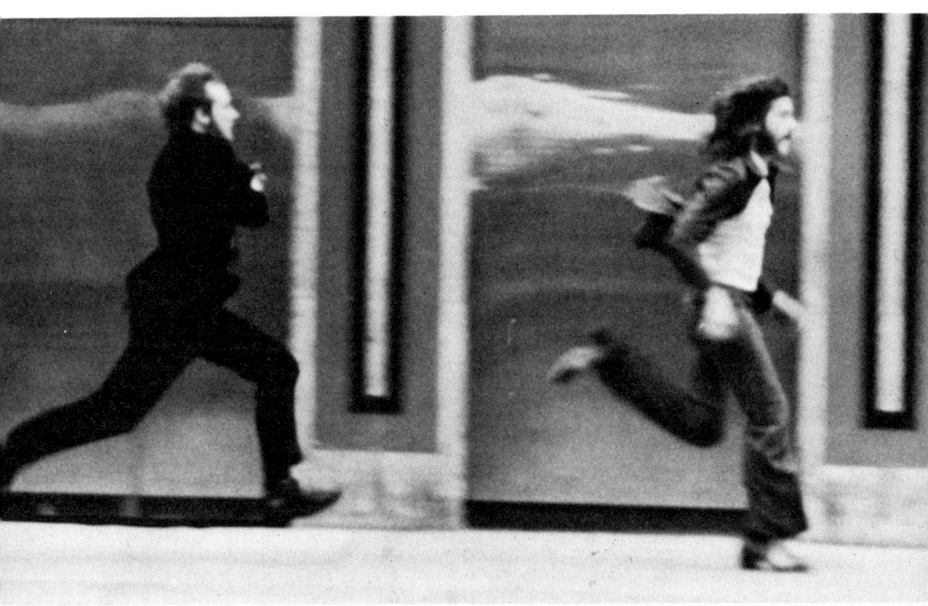

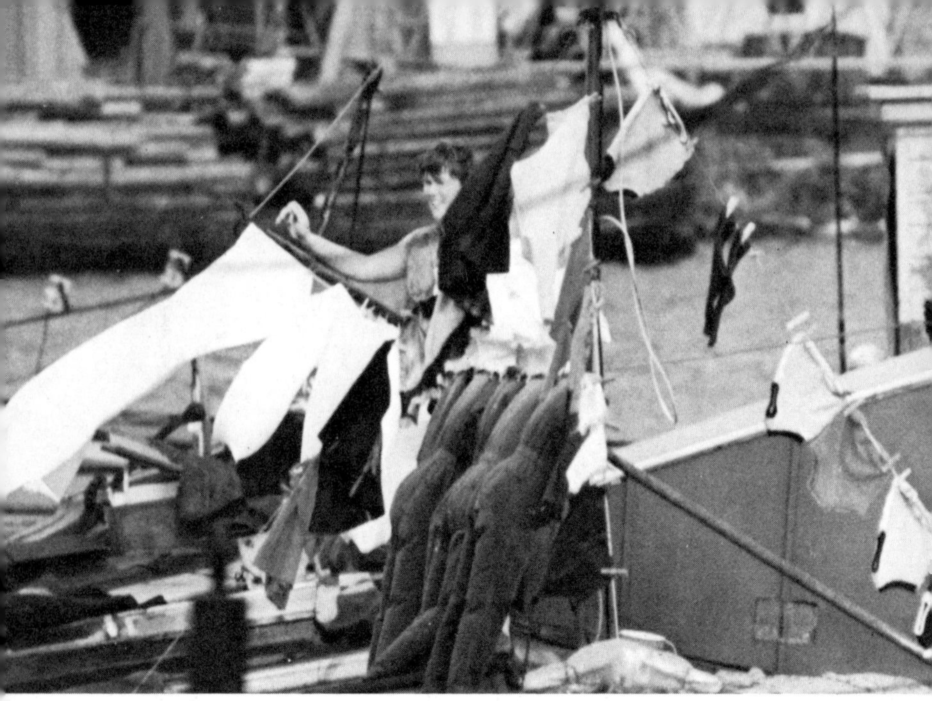

Coveralls filled by a brisk wind on a Dutch barge look like three men hung out to dry. Other clothes look like little ship's signal flags. Taken with a 135 mm lens; 1/500 sec. at f/8.

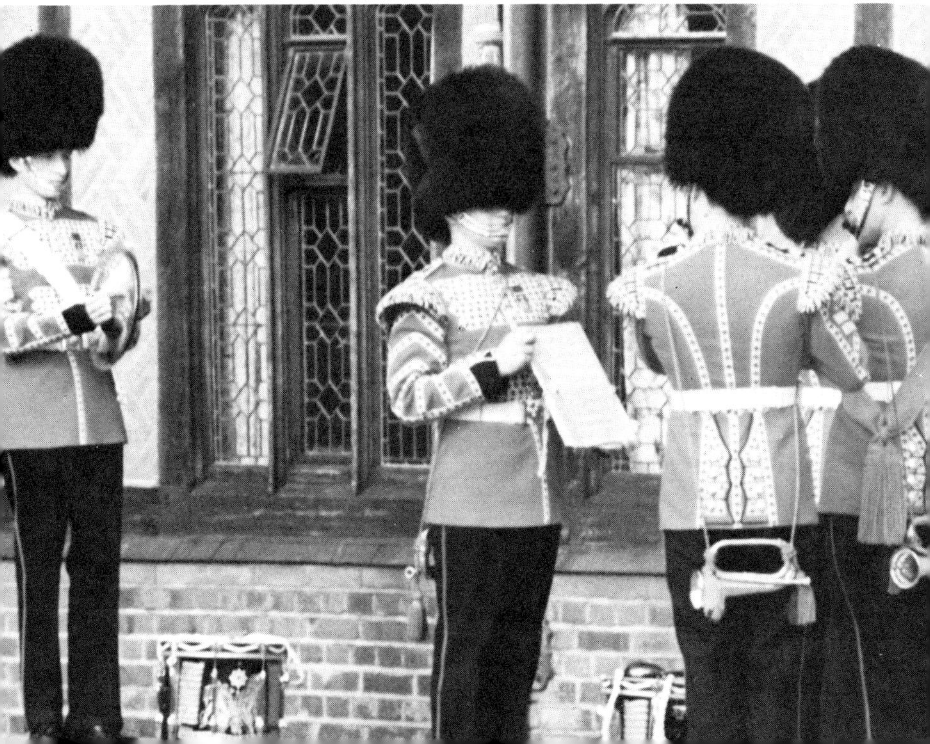

Humor is difficult to show in pictures. This fellow, whose sole job at the moment is to hold music for the fife players, must have the rank of "Music Holder, Second Class." Shot at Windsor Castle with a 50 mm lens; 1/250 sec. at f/8.

A contrived picture of two bandsmen; a very tall tuba player has switched instruments with a very short piccolo player.

A little old lady is feeding the pigeons in Trafalgar Square. One particularly large pigeon is perched squarely on her head.

The list is endless, and if you can sprinkle a few shots like these in with your otherwise serious efforts, you'll have considerable success with your audience.

Candids

You must try to shoot more candids and fewer posed shots. The candids will be alive while the posed ones tend to be static. Such candids make the viewer feel that he is right there, experiencing the scene himself. A good many of the illustrations in this book are candids—but planned ones.

A candid picture can be set up, at least to a degree. You can place yourself where you already have a good-looking picture ready to shoot. Everything is fine, except something is missing—that special point of interest which you must wait for. Soon enough, along will come a person, a car, a bird, or something else that will complete the scene. That's still a candid—but you have directed it from your vantage point. Suppose you are standing near an absolutely beautiful temple in Kyoto, waiting patiently—and along comes a priest just in time to complete your composition. It's still a candid picture, even if you guided things your way until you had just the right scene in your viewfinder.

The cops chasing the robber, described previously, is a true candid. But is it really? The photographer was just sitting there, resting, but he had his camera all set for anything that might happen—which it surely did! It's easy for people to say "You sure were lucky—you were in the right place at the right time." True, but one must be ready and do something about it too.

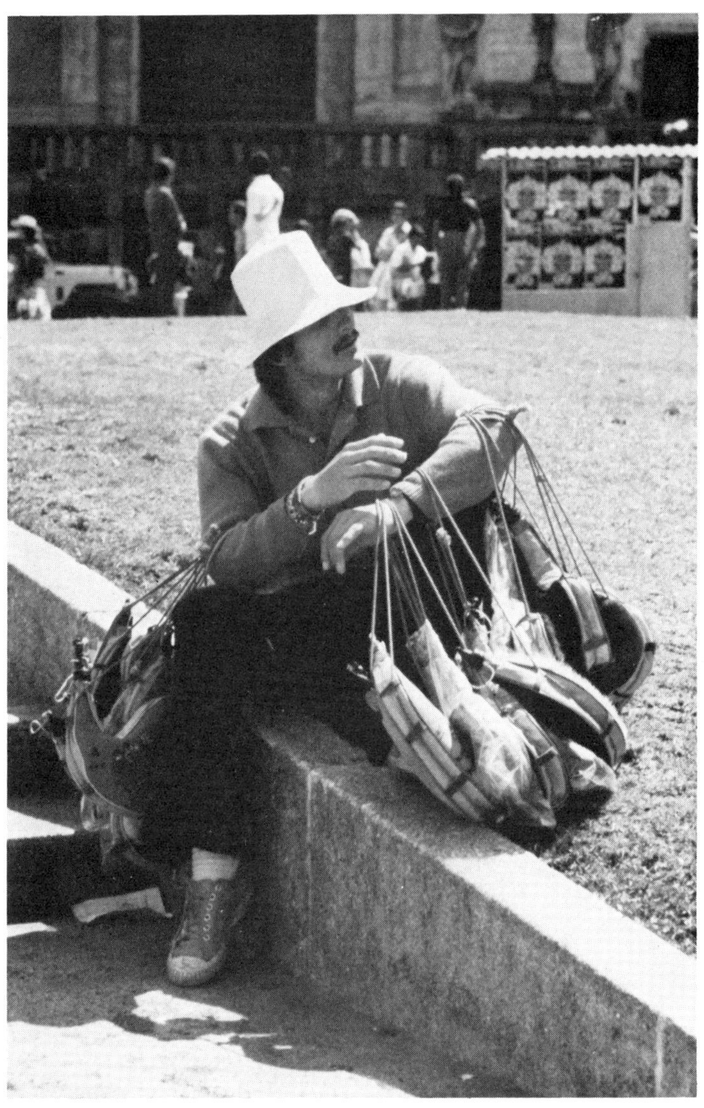

Boata *seller on the morning of the bullfight. No self-respecting* aficionado *would think of attending the bullfight without his* boata, *or wineskin. Taken with a 50 mm lens; 1/500 sec. at f/8.*

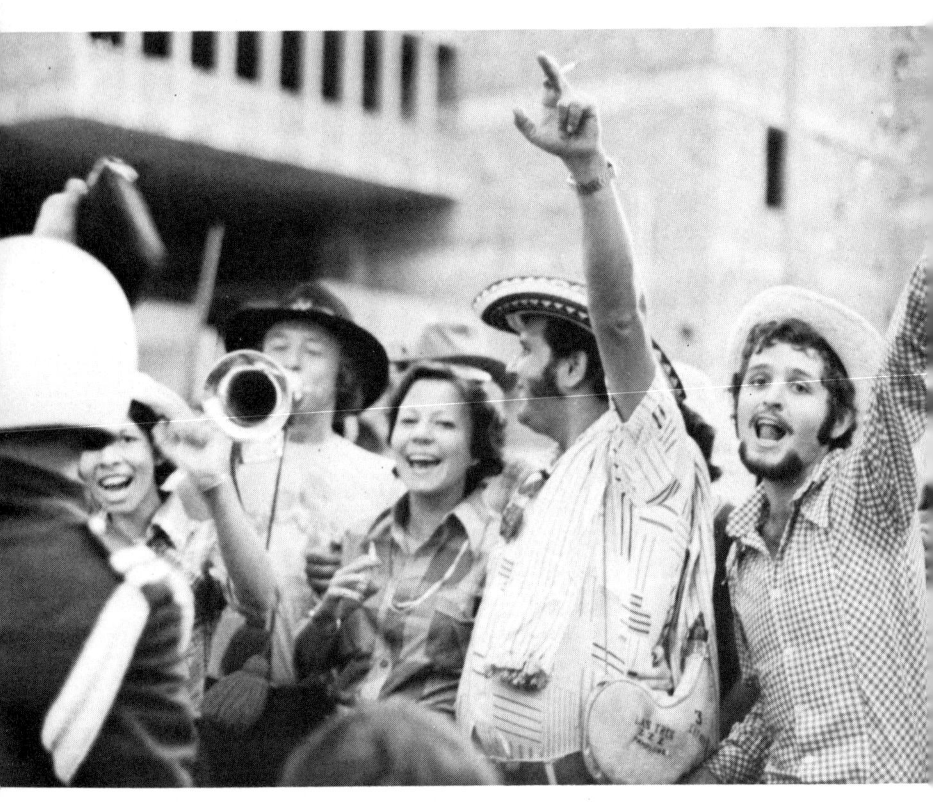

After a full card of bullfights, these fans are full of the excitement of the arena—and not a little of the wine, too. This quick grab shot was made with a 50 mm lens prefocused at six feet with the shutter adjusted to 1/250 sec. The aperture was automatic but was probably about f/4.

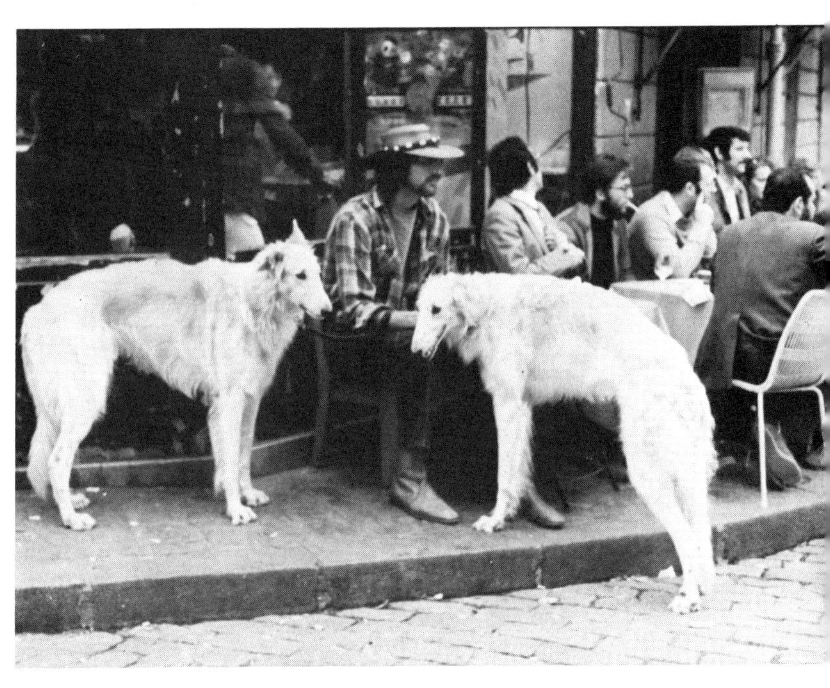

This man, so proud of his matched pair of pedigreed dogs, is otherwise quite alone—even in Paris. Taken with a 50 mm lens; 1/60 sec. at f/5.6.

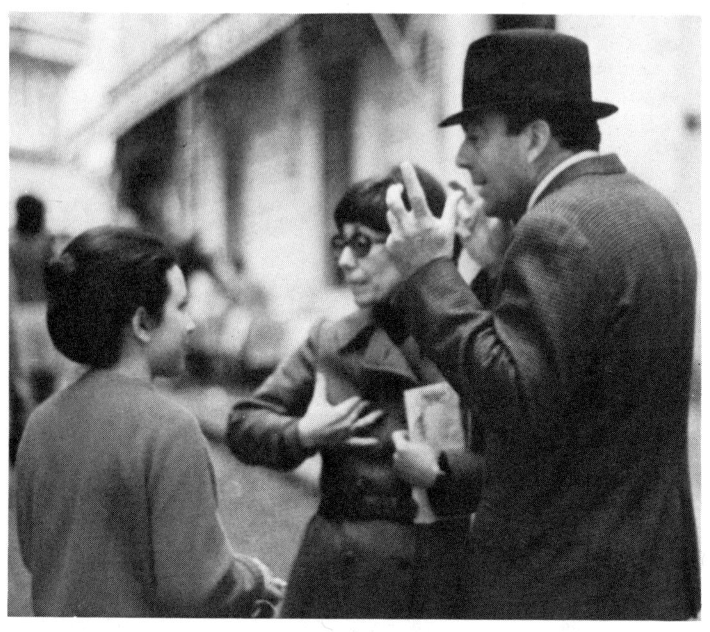

The French are noted for being highly expressive. They talk with their hands. If you're quick with your camera and have it preset and ready to use, you can get pictures like this, taken with a 50 mm lens; 1/250 sec. at f/2.8.

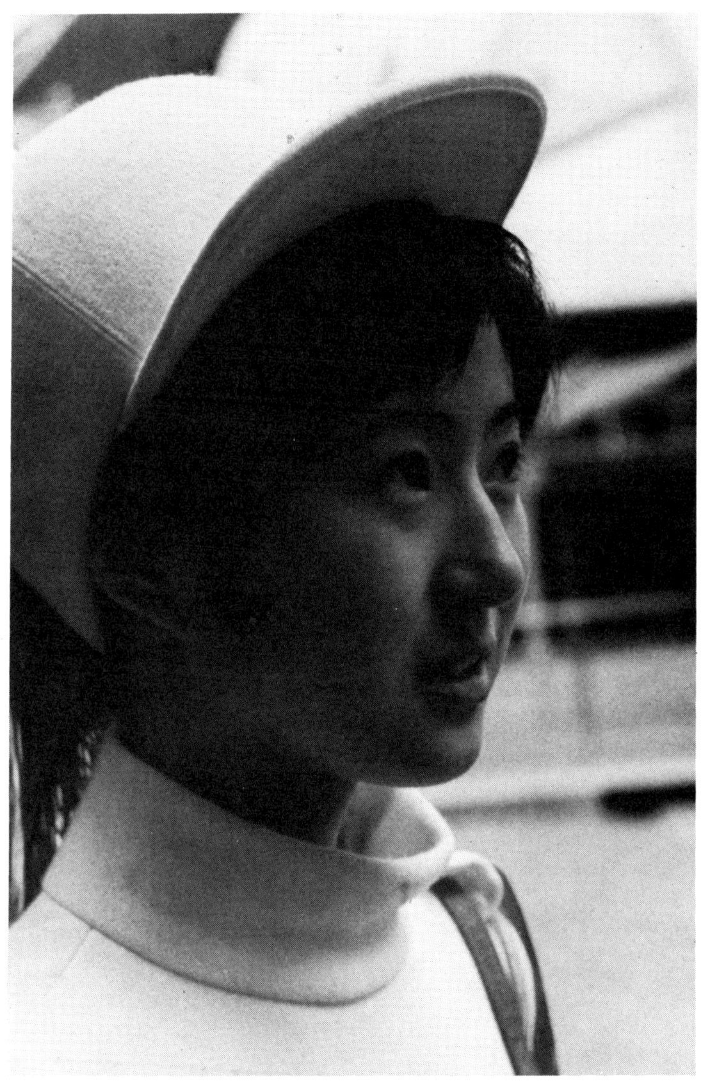

This guide at the Osaka World's Fair made an excellent subject for a candid portrait. Through hand signs, she was asked to turn her head and eyes to the side for a pleasing three-quarter front view. The distracting background was intentionally held out of focus through the use of a short telephoto (135 mm) lens.

This groundskeeper for one of the highly photo-genic temples in Kyoto, Japan, is a fine subject for a picture himself. Taken with a 50 mm lens; 1/250 sec.at f/5.6.

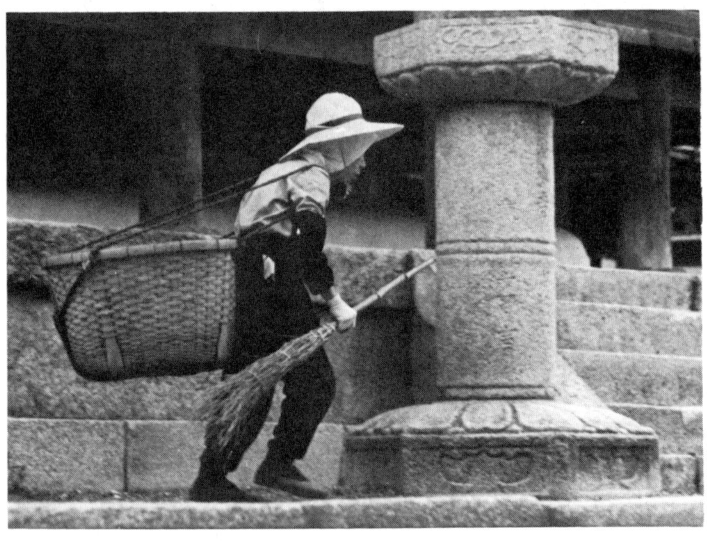

If you don't learn to shoot good candids for your trip, you're going to come home with a set of dull, uninteresting shots that even you will hate. Practice while you're still home. When you're spending that "day" in your home town shooting, pretend that you never saw the place before and get some really good candids for your mini-portfolio. Who knows—the Chamber of Commerce might just jump at the chance to use some of your pictures. When you have finished that day's shooting, carry through by processing all your pictures or having them processed in the same way as you intend having your trip pictures done. Edit those finished pictures down to the ones you think are truly good. Now ask yourself what you are doing right and what you are doing wrong. If you're a severe enough critic (and if you aren't, your spouse or a friend will be), you can't help but learn a lot from your effort.

Police and Military

You will undoubtedly have the good fortune, at least once on your trip, to see a parade. Parades are the photographer's paradise. The uniforms are there just for you and your camera. You can make pictures of shiny brass buttons, colorful tunics, highly polished boots, and ceremonial swords until you're out of film.

If you know ahead of time where the local troops are getting ready for duty or a parade, you can make some splendid pictures. With luck, you might be able to shoot an inspection of the troops before a parade. Wellington Barracks in London offers more photo opportunities when the soldiers are getting ready for the Changing of the Guard than does the actual ceremony itself in front of nearby Buckingham Palace.

When you see someone asking a policeman directions, set up quickly and perhaps you will be able to get a picture of him pointing directions. Policemen directing traffic are great subjects for pictures—especially some of the Italian "conductors" with their batons and their hand

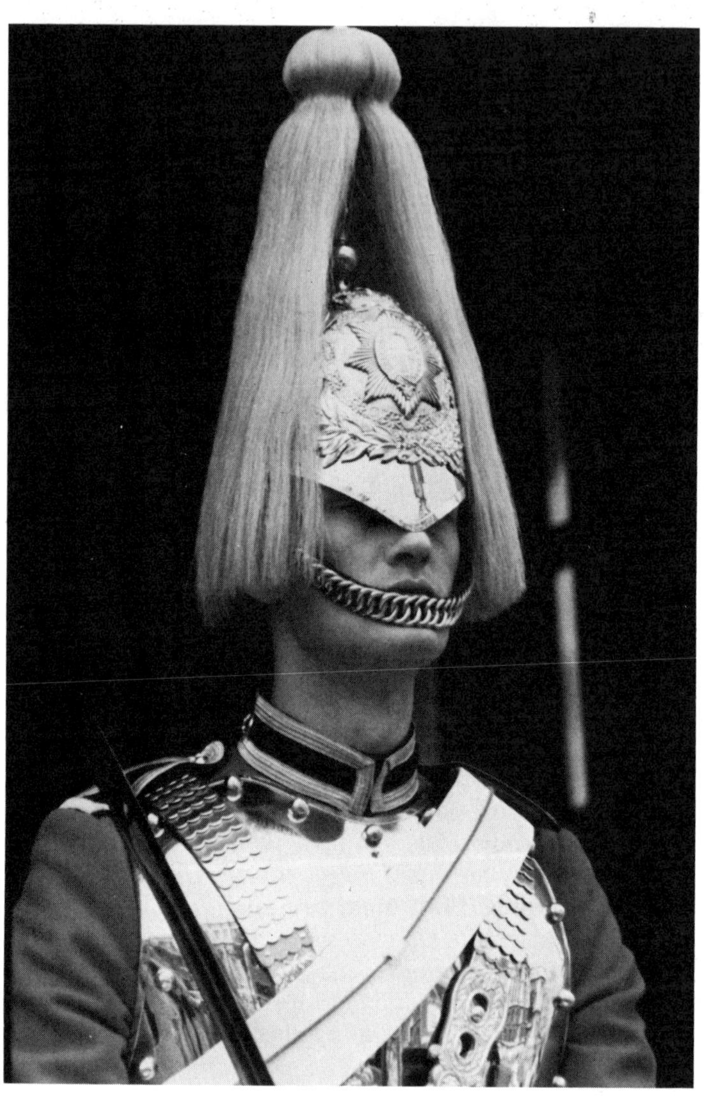

The soldier on duty at London's Horse Guards was so still on his horse that the photographer was able to carefully focus, compose, and even shoot at a fairly slow shutter speed, assuring the sharpest possible portrait. Taken with a 135 mm lens; 1/125 sec. at f/22.

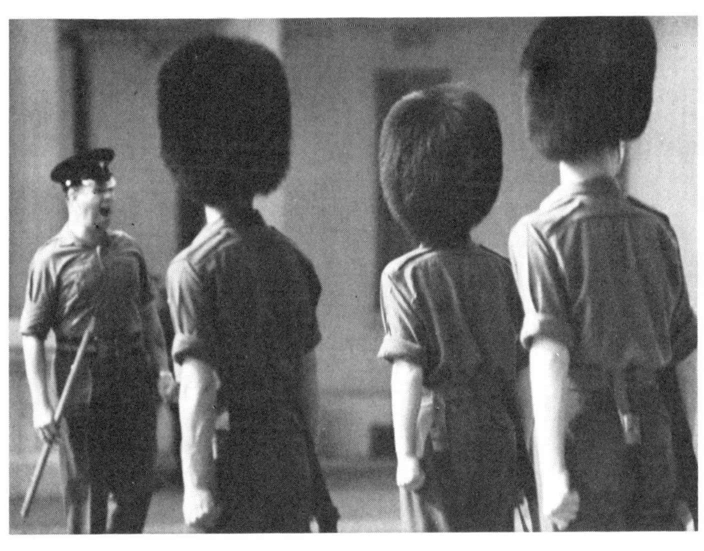

One can almost hear this drill sergeant barking out his commands. These soldiers are practicing at Wellington Barracks for the full-dress Changing of the Guard Ceremony at Buckingham Palace. Taken with a 135 mm lens; 1/250 sec. at f/11.

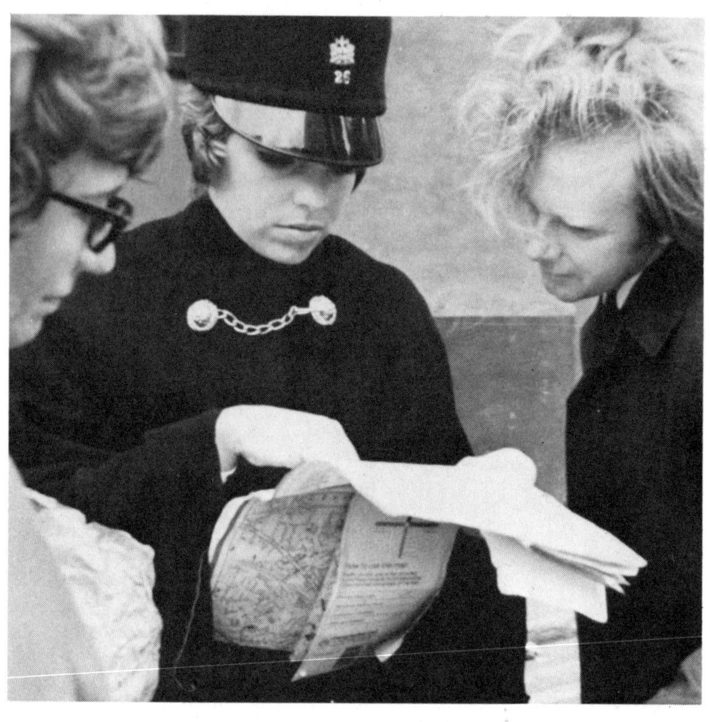

Here is a completely unposed, candid photo of a London police-woman offering assistance to a couple of tourists. The background is plain and the composition is acceptable for a "grab shot." A 135 mm lens was used; automatic aperture at 1/250 sec.

and body motions. They appear to be orchestrating traffic, rather than merely directing it.

Some uniformed people will actually pose for you. Tact and a little subtle flattery will help. Foreign military uniforms are magnificent, and among certain services the men who wear them are deliberately chosen for their stature. Remember that the background should be suitable, so move around your subject until you really have a composition—not just a snapshot.

Mounted policemen or soldiers are ideal subjects. You might see an exhibition of horsemanship such as show jumping or dressage. Remember always to make each picture tell where it was taken, and don't waste film on something you could photograph at home.

THE COUNTRYSIDE

Landscapes

One major photographic subject of your trip will probably be landscapes. Having done research on this subject, you will know quite a few places to seek out. Every country has its famous scenes, and you should try to visit some of these for the benefit of your camera. But while you're there, keep your eyes open for other less-well-known scenes that will also make excellent landscapes.

Hedgerows in Europe immediately tell the viewer that he isn't looking at an Iowa farm. Place a thatched-roof cottage in the scene and you have a winner. But wait—half a mile away and heading right into the scene is a two-wheeled cart, drawn by a tired old horse. Be patient. Wait for the cart to move into just the right place in your composition and you'll have everything going for you. You have plenty of time to check your exposure and the composition. Are there some puffy white clouds in the sky? Can you make these a part of your total composition? Now you're getting the idea!

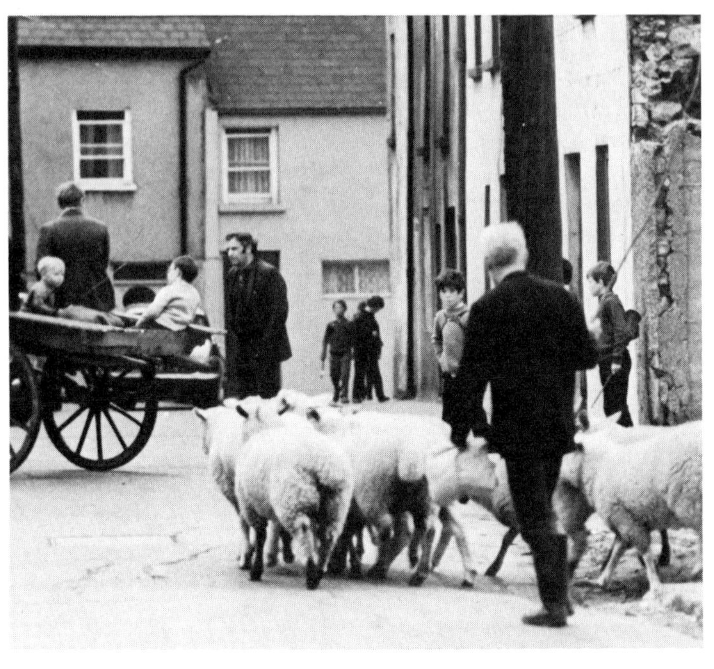

The two-wheeled cart, the sheep being driven through the streets—these are familiar sights in Ireland. Taken with a 135 mm lens; 1/250 sec. at f/5.6.

One thing to look for: When you have finished making a picture of this sort, ask yourself if the sky is the brightest part of the scene. If so, you've done something wrong. You should have darkened the sky with a filter or possibly even cropped it out entirely. There are ways to

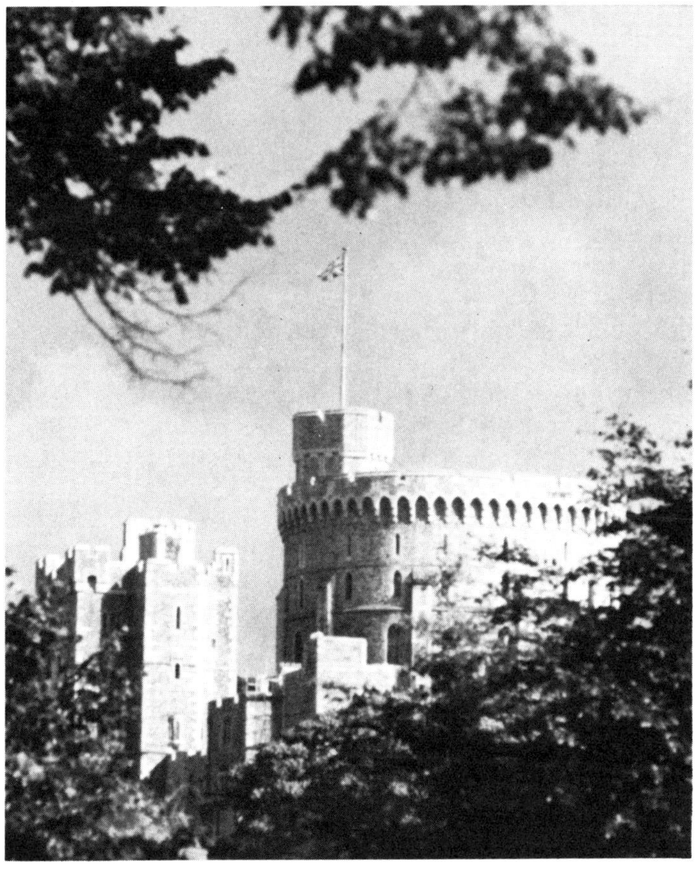

Windsor Castle as seen from the River Thames. Although the sun is shining on the Round Tower, there is a storm on the way. The frame of trees around the tower adds interest to the composition. Taken with a 135 mm lens; 1/250 sec. at f/5.6.

make everything fall into place for that one great picture—
if you'll just plan ahead.

Whatever you do, don't just shoot dead landscapes.
Give them some life in one way or another. Have some
point for the eye to rest on in the finished picture. This
could be a church spire in the distance, or a little village,
or even a single bird in the sky. Whatever you can find to
add life to your landscapes will be worth while.

Farms

Look for farms that are different from those at home.
While the livestock will be the same, the barnyard and
farm equipment will be different. You may even see some
old-fashioned tools that would add special interest to your
pictures.

Some countries have programs that allow tourists to
stay at a farm, taking all meals there and experiencing the
good feeling of being in a rural setting. Whether or not you
are put to work will depend on the individual program.
Don't forget to photograph the people along with their
tools and surroundings.

Canals

The old industrial canals or waterways were often
the best means of transporting goods before the railways
were built. They are still highly interesting manmade
features of many countries. While some canals are no
longer in working order as they not needed, others still
carry considerable commercial traffic. In some places
where commerical use has disappeared, local boating
enthusiasts have restored old canals for pleasure boating
with great success.

Until you have floated down one of these lovely
waterways at a leisurely three miles (5 kilometres) per
hour, finding a new vista at each turning, you don't know
what true peace is. Occasionally, when you find your

canal paralleling one of the high-speed expressways, you will begin to realize that all of us are forever speeding from one place to another, never taking time to really see anything. On a canal, you have time to see and photograph everything.

You can live the experience of winding the paddles of a lock and helping work the boat through these watery "steps" up and down hills. For pictures, there are many subjects: lockkeepers' houses, canal pubs, old horse-drawn long boats, the lock equipment, signs, and the people who still travel the waterways, living on their boats year-round. There are literally thousands of miles of canals throughout the world, many of them lovely and all of them interesting in some way.

CITIES

Buildings

For some reason, people think they must photograph every famous building in every city they visit. This can result in some very boring photography. However, there are ways to add interest to the most hackneyed scenes. For example, No. 10 Downing Street is an ordinary-looking building—just like so many other government buildings in London. But—the Foreign Office, across the street, has a large gateway through which sleek official cars can pass. Frame your picture of No. 10 by backing into this opening. Further interest could be added by including one or two of the London policemen who usually stand guard in front of the Prime Minister's residence. The point is, if you must shoot a building like this one, at least try to make your finished picture interesting.

There are plenty of scenes in the cities and towns of the world that are of much greater photographic value. Always consider your city views not as pictures of individual buildings but as compositions of buildings, as elements of your composition. A group of buildings can offer quite an interesting arrangement if you look at them with the eye of an artist, rather than that of an engineer. You can balance the thin with the fat, the tall with the short, the light with the dark. The Arch of Triumph in Paris is not, by itself, really much to look at. But a long-lens shot through this same arch down the Champs-Elysées can be breathtaking.

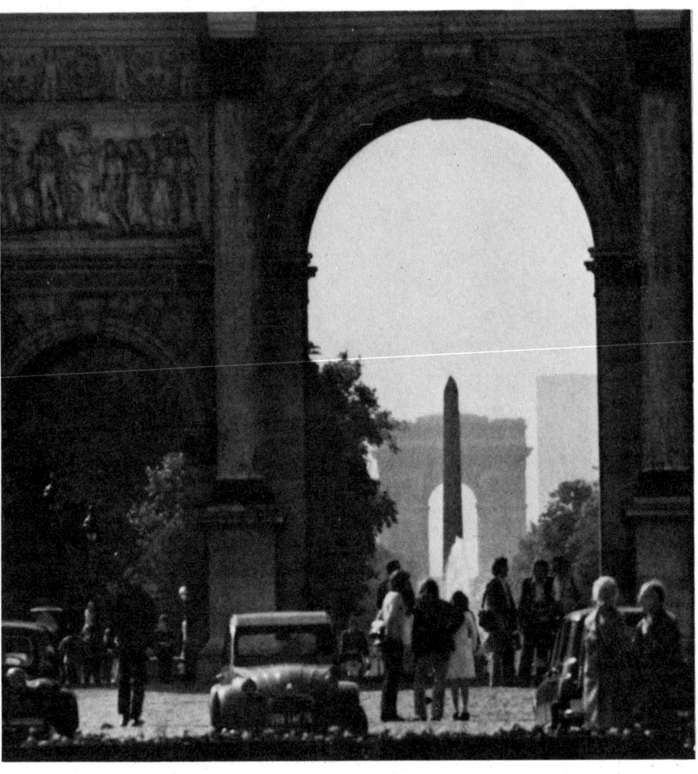

The Arc de Triomphe and the Obélisque as seen through the Arc du Carrousel in Paris. This often-photographed juxtaposition of monuments must be photographed with a stopped-down tele-photo lens (on a tripod) for the great depth of field required. Taken with a 300 mm lens; 1/125 sec. at f/16.

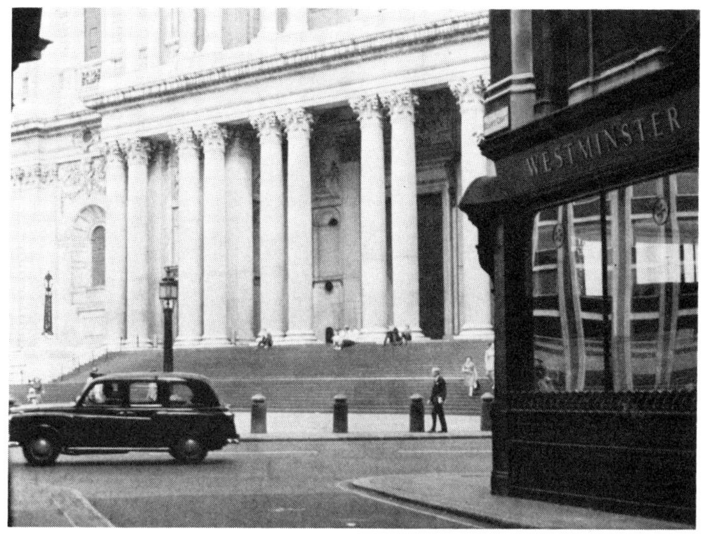

*This unusual view of a much-photgraphed London landmark—
St. Paul's Cathedral—was taken from a little side street. Always
look for similar unusual ways to shoot the usual subjects. Taken
with a 50 mm lens; 1/250 sec. at f/5.6.*

Details of Buildings. Rather than photograph an entire building, try to move in close for a choice detail that will reflect the spirit of what the architect was saying. The play of light and shadow upon such segments of buildings can produce lovely effects. Single doors or windows are fair game for your lens. Moving closer, doorknobs make a wonderful study.

Highviews. If you are one of those people with the compulsion to climb to the top of every monument, tower, cathedral, tree, bridge, or whatever high point you see, put it to work on your trip. By making high shots of the places you visit, you can better show your experiences through

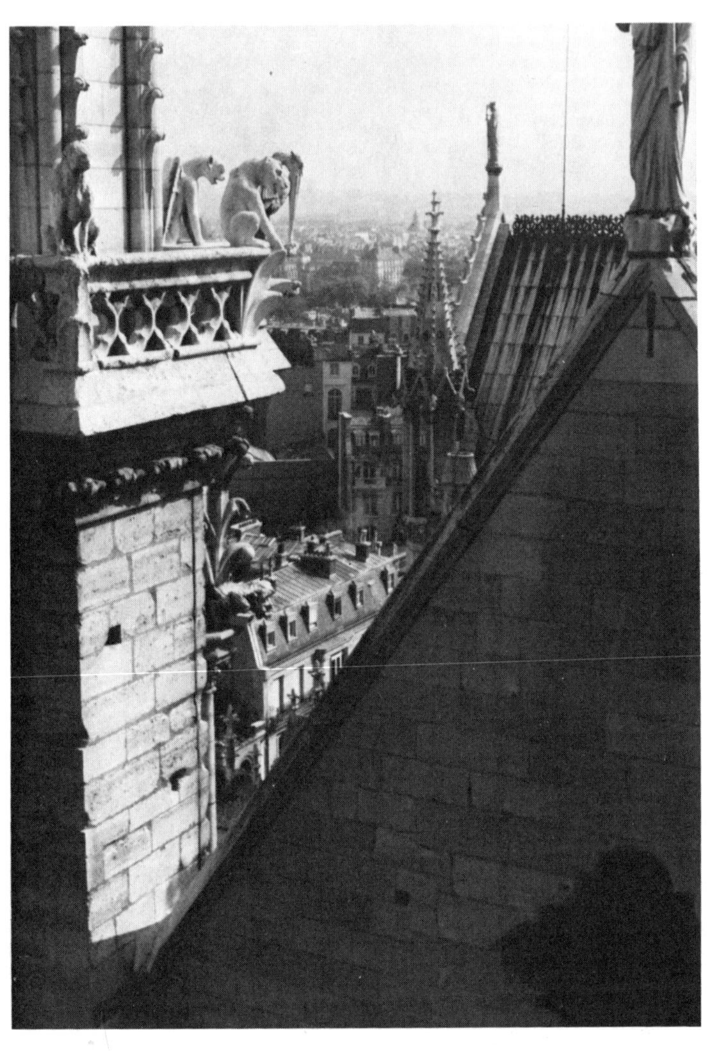

This shot of the rooftops of Paris and the
famous gargoyles of Notre Dame Cathedral
was made only after a climb of many,
many steps. Taken with a 50 mm lens;
1/125 sec. at f/11.

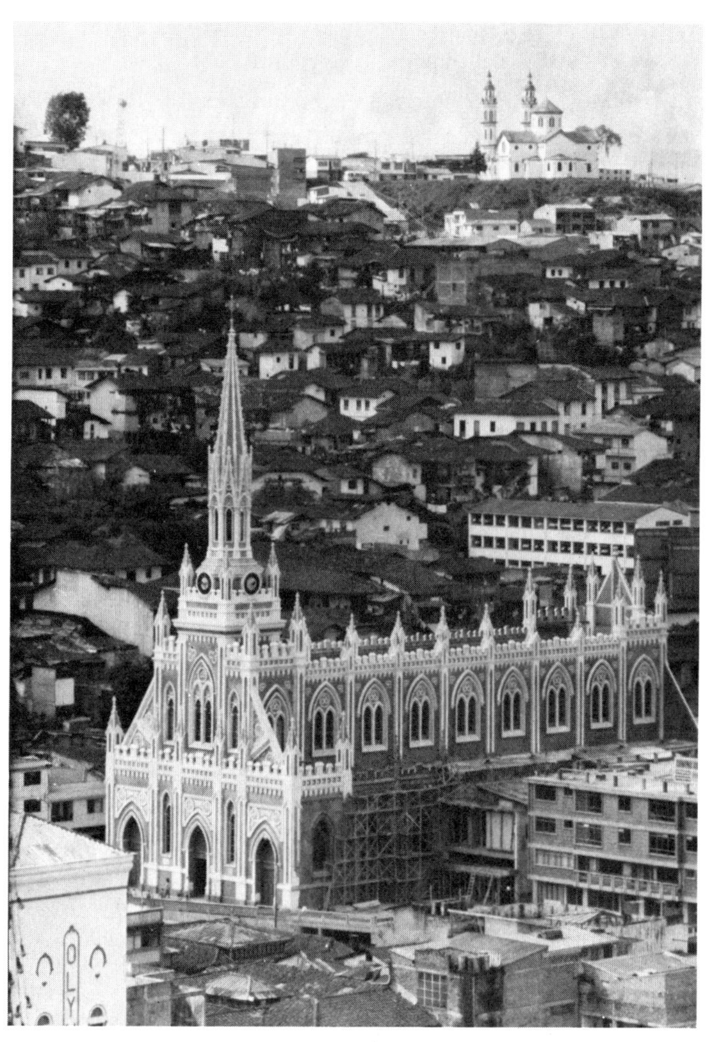

This unusual high view of two churches in
Manazales, Colombia, was made from the
top of the city's cathedral. A 135 mm
lens was used here to isolate just what the
photographer wanted to show in the picture.
Taken at 1/125 sec. at f/8.

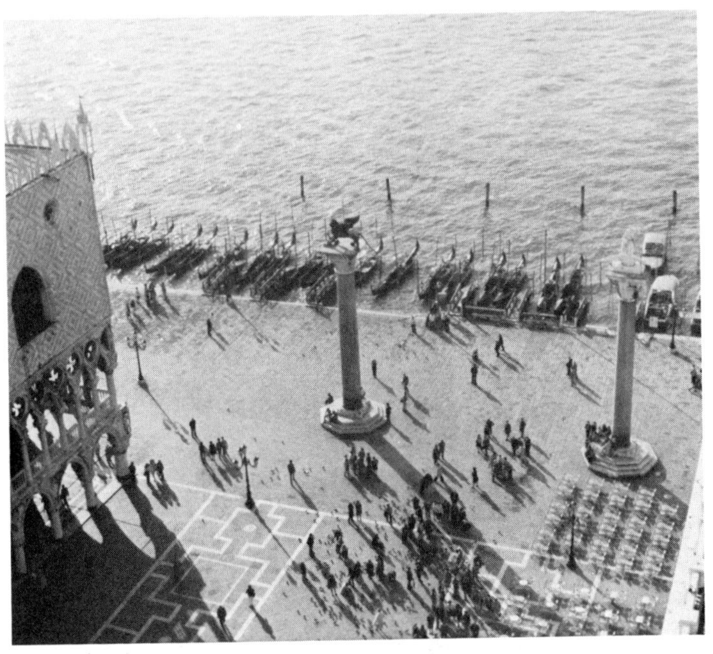

This high shot was made from the top of the Campanile, 300 feet above Piazza San Marco in Venice. The wide-angle (24 mm) lens took in the whole scene: the two famous columns, the facade of the Doge's Palace (at left), a line of gondolas, and a crowd of people—all backlighted. Taken at 1/250 sec. at f/11;

your pictures. This will add a new perspective to your portfolio of places you have visited.

Let's say you are in Amsterdam and have been shooting for two or three days. At last, you have an opportunity to climb to the top of the Old Church. The city is very flat, as is all of the Netherlands, and a high look is worth seeing. From the Old Church, you can see clear to the outskirts of the city. You can also see a lot of details in the central part of town that aren't visible at ground level.

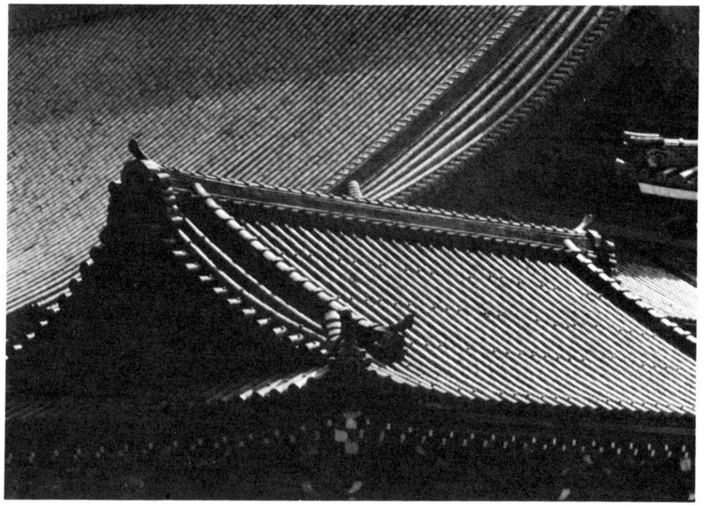

Detail of one of the wonderful rooftops of a temple in Kyoto, Japan. By keeping the composition tight, there is no sky in the picture to detract by its brightness from the pattern of tiles and lines. Taken with a 135 mm lens; 1/250 sec. at f/16.

By first making a series of wide-angle views in different directions, you will be able later to identify and locate anything you subsequently shoot in detail. Remember to tip your camera or exposure meter downward slightly in making your meter reading. Otherwise, the light-sensing cell will be seeing a lot of bright sky and the resulting exposure will be affected.

After making the wide views from above, switch to a short telephoto lens to shoot individual buildings or small groups of them, canal views, and even street scenes down below—all from your single perch.

When you have used your short telephoto lens to full advantage, switch to your standard or normal focal length lens and another whole world will open up for you. It is amazing what a different lens can do.

Try to shoot straight down at people walking on the street—traffic policemen, street sweepers, and anything else that moves. Are there any rooftops in view that make interesting patterns? You could spend a morning or an afternoon doing this one scene if you didn't have to move on to other places. It's worth it, though.

At high vantage points, atmospheric haze must be considered. While you may not be that high up, you will be in position to see and photograph long distances, and this is where haze becomes a problem. A haze filter does not cut haze, as many have been led to believe. All it does is filter out some of the ultraviolet light that produces the blueish color in slides. The haze is still there, though. If you are using color negative film, the haze filter is useless. Just shoot and make your correction in the darkroom. Better yet, let the blueish haze remain and try to get something very colorful in the foreground of your pictures. This will give an illusion of depth. The same goes for industrial haze or smog in the cities. Quite often in picture-taking, you can put problem situations to work in your favor if you will just think about them a little bit.

Close-ups. It is easy to get so wrapped up in what you are doing with your camera that you forget to photograph the most obvious things. While you are making pictures of buildings, trees, bridges, and myriad other subjects, be sure to move in close now and then for detail shots and even extreme close-ups.

While it may not have occurred to you, your best close-up lens is actually your wide-angle lens. With your normal focal length lens—and even more so with the longer lenses—the closer you go to a subject, the more

*Close-up of carved wooden doors on the Town Hall of
the French village of Nemours. By having a friend
point a finger at the lovely little figure, it was possible
to indicate the scale. The wide-angle lens (here, a
24 mm) is great for close-ups, because at a given
distance and image size depth of field is always
greater; this allows hand-held shooting at reasonably
fast shutter speeds and at reasonably large apertures.
This was taken at 1/125 sec. at f/5.6.*

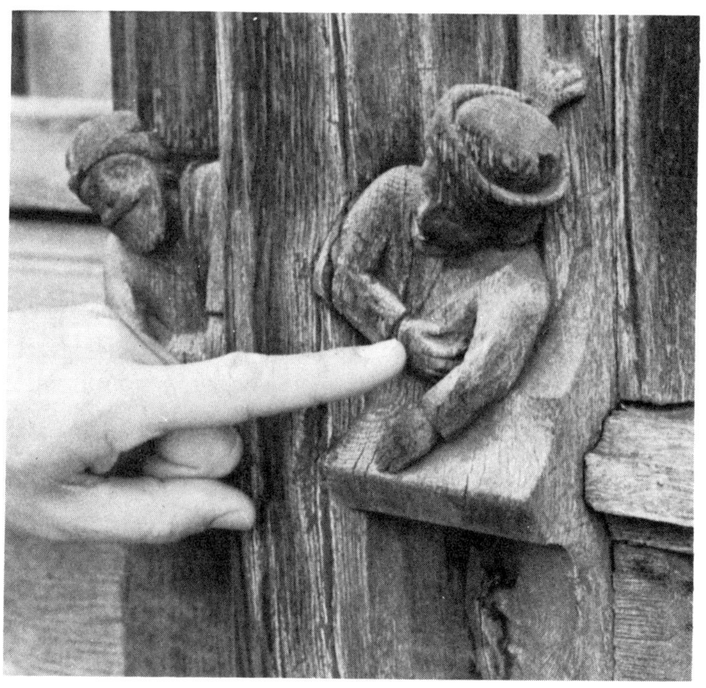

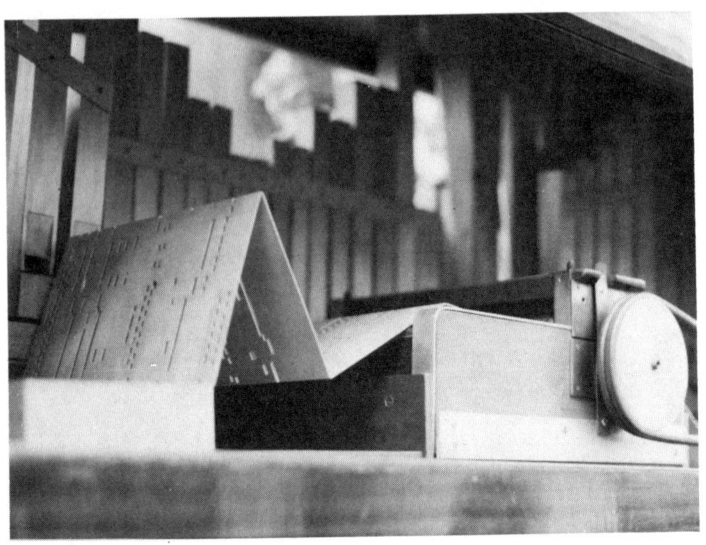

At first glance this looks like a child's toy. In fact, it is the inner workings of a Dutch barrel organ. It works like a player piano: the flat pages of a "book" of music unfold and are pulled across openings through which compressed air is allowed to flow. This wonderful contraption is seen on many streets of the Netherlands. The close-up was shot with a 50 mm lens; f/2.8 at 1/60 sec.

limited will be your depth of field. The wide-angle lens, however, offers a much greater depth of field for any given *f*-stop. In fact, if you close your lens down a couple of *f*-stops from wide open, your depth will be incredible.

If you are photographing around a really old building, move in close for a look at the very old woodwork or stonework. Little signs set into the old walls are just asking to be photographed up close.

In Ireland a horse pulling a cart is wearing a funny hat. Quickly put your long lens on and get a close-up of him with his ears jutting through the holes his owner has provided for them.

As you pass the city prison, you see a man's hand projecting through the bars. With your long lens, photograph just a hand and bars. Can you make a good composition? Is he calling for help—or is he just getting a partial suntan?

When you shoot close-ups, keep your pictures simple. Don't clutter them with too many details. Only show what you want the viewer to see—nothing else. Then the eye must move to the one place you want it to go—the center of interest.

After enjoying an opera or a fine concert, group your ticket stubs, program, and whatever else you can find—such as a newspaper advertisement for the show— and shoot a close-up of this collage.

Shiny brass door knockers, knobs, hinges, and other brightly polished hardware make fine close-ups, as do boat riggings and fittings. What about the kitchen of that nice little restaurant you have just enjoyed? The owners would be proud if you were to ask to make such pictures. Once you're in there, you will find lots of close-up material, including shots of that good food being prepared. You might even get an extra dessert or a bottle of wine for your interest.

When you are able to see folk dancers performing, take the usual pictures, for you have excellent subjects. Then move in close for a shot of the dancers' simple sandals, their traditional hats, and the hand-woven fabrics of their costumes.

When you are visiting the local flower markets, move in close for shots of the lovely blooms. Now try something different: Use your wide-angle for a close-up with a famous landmark in the background. By stopping down your lens and using a slow shutter speed, you can keep everything in focus even at this extreme depth. A shot of a lovely rose with one of the castles on the Rhine River for a background makes a magnificent picture.

Flea Markets offer endless possibilities for close-up pictures. Old brass—polished and otherwise—shouldn't

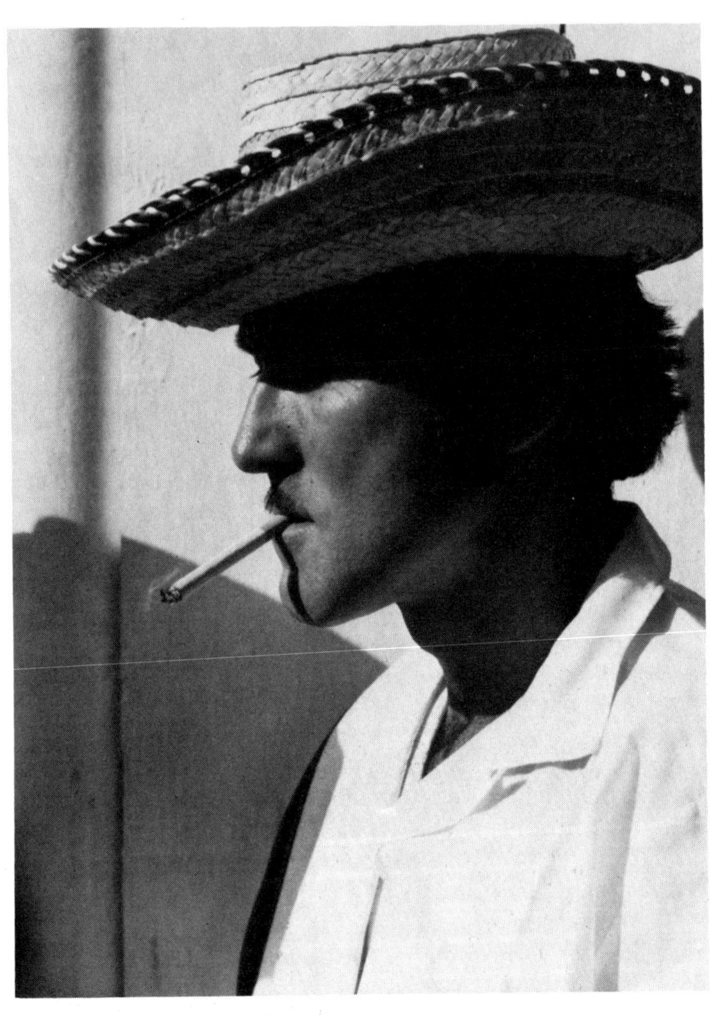

This folk dancer's traditional costume couldn't have been better for this picture. The cigarette completes an already good, simple composition. Taken with a 135 mm lens; 1/250 sec. at f/16.

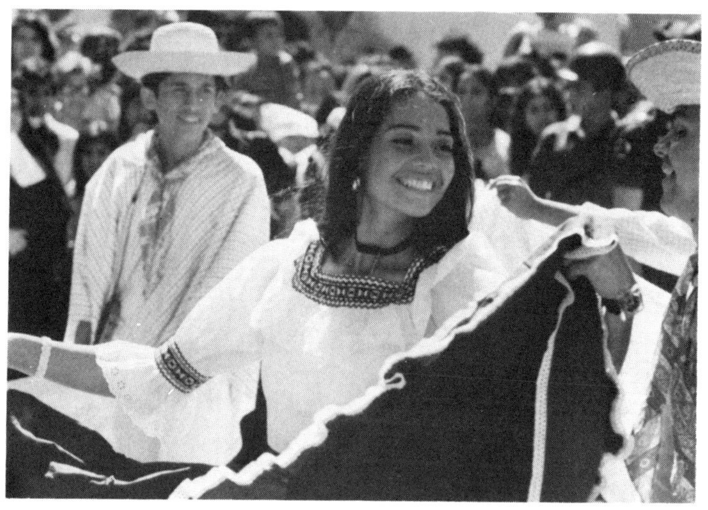

Folk dancers in San Cristobal, Venezuela. Motion suggested by the skirt makes this picture live, as does the dazzling smile. Taken with a 50 mm lens; 1/1000 sec. at f/5.6.

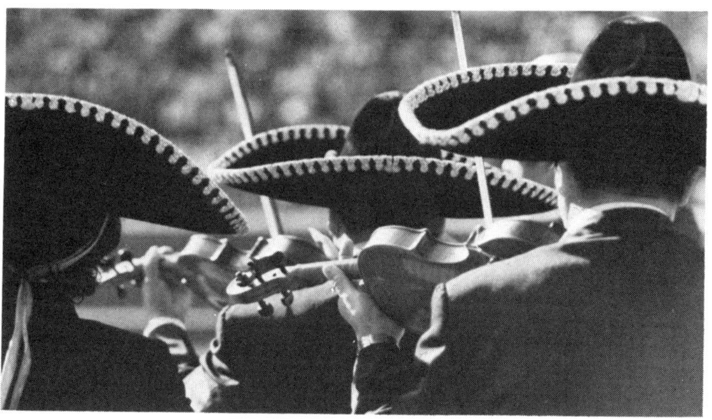

An unusual angle may make an interesting composition. The hats and violins are all the props needed to set the stage for this shot of a mariachi band. Taken with a 135 mm lens; 1/250 sec. at f/16.

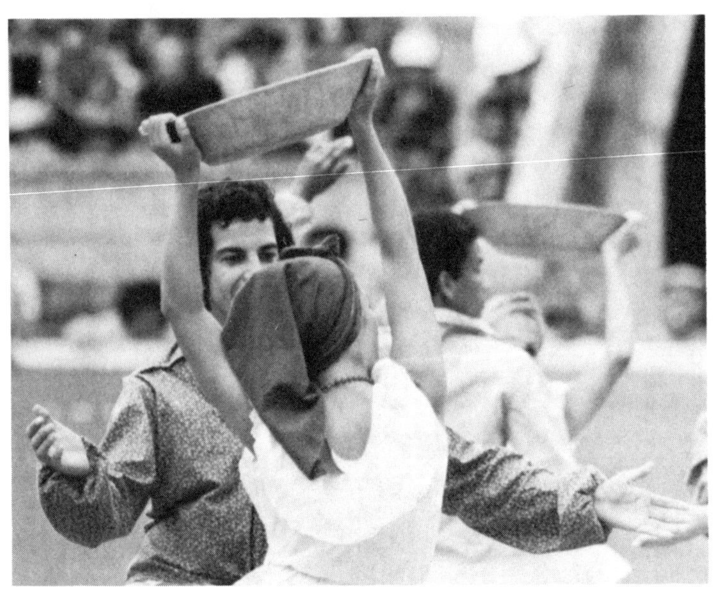

By carefully isolating one couple out of a group of folk dancers, the photographer was able to direct attention exactly where he wanted. Taken with a 135 mm lens; 1/250 sec. at f/5.6.

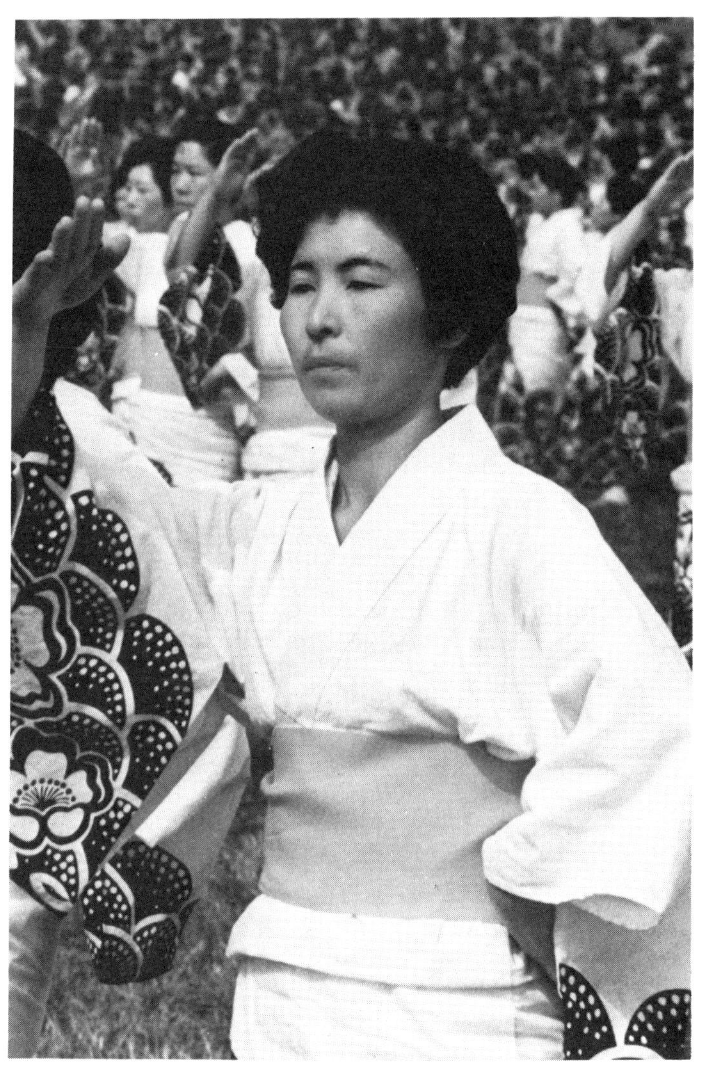

*Traditional Japanese folk dancer wears
a costume that hasn't changed for centuries.
Here is an ideal travel study for any
camera. Taken with a 135 mm lens;
1/500 sec. at f/5.6.*

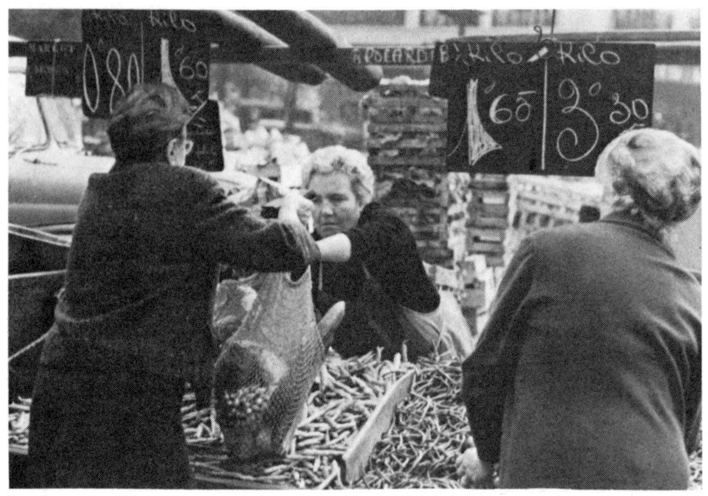

If you keep your camera ready at all times, you will be rewarded with pictures such as this one. Taken at one of the many street markets in Paris, this shot has it all—produce, seller, and buyer—plus hand-printed or chalked price signs. The camera was fitted with a 50 mm lens and exposure was adjusted ahead of time to 1/250 sec. at f/5.6. It was also prefocused and shot from the waist.

be overlooked. Broken dolls, old clothing, war medals, and all the odds and ends to be found here are great material for the close-up lens. Remember to isolate carefully so that you have a single center of interest in your pictures.

Points of Interest

Cathedrals. Europe and Latin America, in particular, are full of cathedrals representing centuries of architectural history. All of them are large, and make excellent subjects for a wide-angle lens. Inside and outside, you'll be working that lens overtime.

Because of the very low level of lighting inside, you will want to steady your camera either on a tripod or at least on something solid and, preferably, level. Fortunately, a tripod may not be necessary. Nearly every large building has some sort of chair, bench, or table upon which you can position your camera for time exposures. A one-second exposure will usually suffice.

Vertical pictures are a little bit more difficult, but they can also be made. By placing your camera against the rear wall and holding it there, you can be assured of no movement for your time exposure.

While you're in the cathedral, be sure to find out if it is possible to climb to the bell-tower for a panoramic view of the surrounding city. Often this is possible, and the climb is always worth it.

Whatever you do, don't come home with identical pictures of each cathedral you have visited. Try to do something a little bit different each time. Close-ups, pictures looking straight up at the ceiling, shots of the mosaic floor, details of wood carvings, statuary, stained-glass windows all make superb photographic subjects.

Castles and Ruins. Most people who have been raised on fairy tales will be disappointed at their first sight of a real castle. Most of them are in ruins, and it takes a fair amount of imagination to see them as they appear in the legends of King Arthur and the Round Table. With a few exceptions, there aren't all that many famous castles. But when you travel around the world, you will see a lot of them, from the craggy seaside rockpiles brooding over the stormy Irish Sea to the ruined fortifications of Norman crusaders in the barren hills of the Holy Land.

How do you convey the dank smell of centuries that permeates every castle you visit? How do you bring to life the filth and the pageantry of an era centuries dead?

Here are a few suggestions for photographing those venerable ruins. Shoot close-ups of initials carved into the stone walls of the dungeons where prisoners were held.

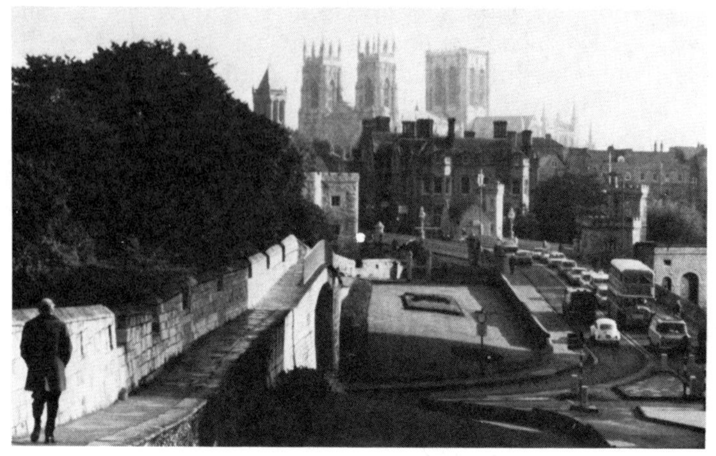

York Minster—the cathedral seen from the ancient wall that nearly surrounds the city even today. A walk on these battlements is a walk into history. The photographer waited for the figure in the foreground to move into exactly the right place to make the composition come alive. Taken with a 50 mm lens; 1/500 sec. at f/16.

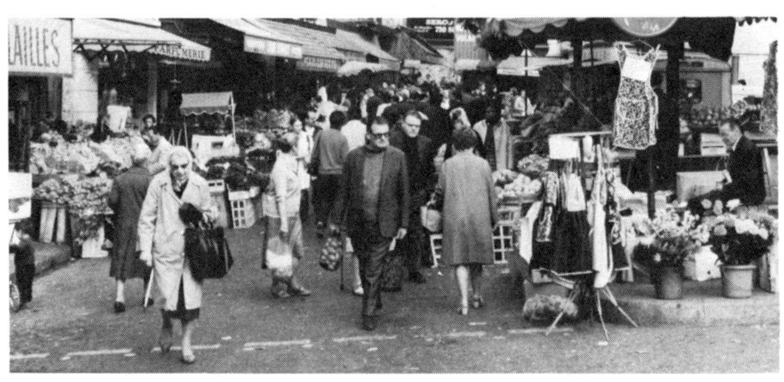

Rue Moufetard is one of the oldest and most picturesque street markets in Paris. At first look, you'd think it was set up just for you and your camera. Taken with a 50 mm lens; 1/125 sec. at f/11.

Make pictures looking through the deep, deep window openings (with bars, of course) to show the massive thickness of the walls. Take long shots showing the site, with the castle as a small part of the composition. Photograph the entrance with portcullis and drawbridge, turrets with old lead or stone roofs, sidelighted texture of stonework, courtyards with old oxcarts or other authentic items that add color, worn stone steps, battlements with view through stonework of the countryside beyond, stone carvings set into the wall, grass growing out of the old cannons.

Flower Markets. Everywhere in the world, people love flowers. Why else would you find so many flower markets wherever you travel? Whatever the reason, these markets are very picturesque.

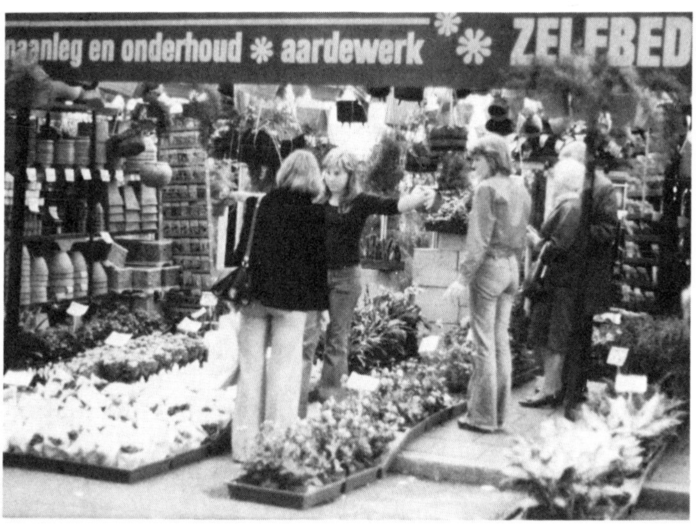

This is a flower market in the center of Amsterdam. The salesgirl seems to be telling her customer that she can deliver a plant "this big." Such figures in action can really bring your pictures to life. Taken with a 50 mm lens; 1/125 sec. at f/8.

The customers at the flower markets, as well as the people who work there, are all great picture subjects. They all have a common love of beauty, and it shows. They are so intent on the buying and selling of beautiful blooms that they never seem to notice photographers. If they do notice, perhaps they are secretly pleased to be photographed amid all that beauty.

Flower buyers are young and old, handsome and ugly; they arrive on bicycles, in trucks, in taxis, and even in limousines. The flower sellers are also worth stalking with the camera. When you see a fine old lady selling an armful of roses to a young man, you wonder where those flowers are going—to his wife, his mother, his sweetheart? Or the proud old man who buys a single bloom and walks away holding it as though he has just bought a most valuable jewel. They're all at the flower market; and all for free for you and your camera.

Fountains. Everywhere you go, you will see fountains. Most are unsightly things and you wonder why in the world they were ever made. But those few that do catch your eye are certainly worth a couple of pictures.

A most important consideration when you are photographing a fountain is the lighting. Move around the fountain until you find the best possible angle. Since there is water movement, consider your shutter speed. Do you want to "freeze" the water or would you like your picture to suggest motion through the use of a slightly slower shutter speed?

Under the right conditions, backlighting can be most effective when you are making fountain pictures. The water seems to come alive with the many reflections created with this sort of lighting. Combine backlighting with a cross-star filter on your lens for an effect of hundreds of stars of varying sizes. The result is dazzling.

Another filter to consider when photographing fountains is the polarizer. With black-and-white or color,

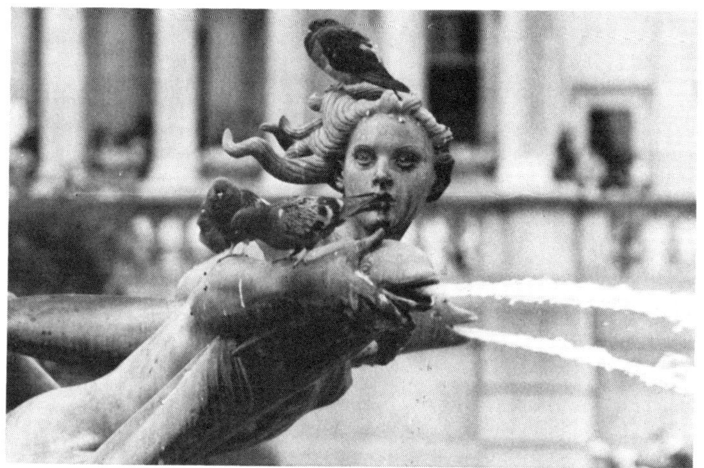

Look for a variety of fountains on your travels. If birds want to get into the act, so much the better. Keep the pictures simple and uncluttered. This one was photographed in London's Trafalgar Square with a 135 mm lens; 1/250 sec. at f/8.

this filter will greatly darken the sky and make the water really stand out. To allow some reflected light to pass through the polarizer rather than be completely absorbed, rotate the filter until you have the effect you want.

Many fountains are adorned with flamboyant, baroque statuary. The water playing over these figures is almost incidental, but a necessary part of the composition. Remember to keep the picture simple and uncluttered. Nothing in the background should distract from the center of interest. Show only what you want—nothing more.

Gateways. Occasionally you will encounter fine old gateways through which you can photograph the buildings beyond. The accompanying photograph of the palace of Fontainebleau was taken through such a gateway. Such a technique can yield dramatic results.

Statues. If you think there are a lot of fountains about, just try counting the statues! There are statues of

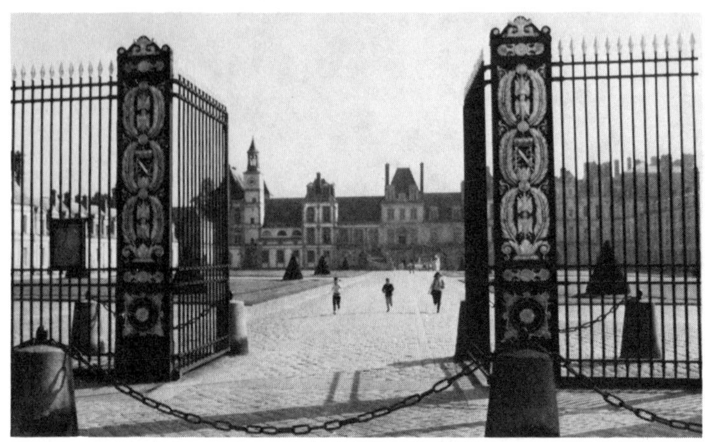

The front of a building might look better if photographed through an open gate or archway. This view of the chateau of Fontainebleau is enhanced in such a way. The running children add vitality to this otherwise static scene. Taken with a 24 mm lens; 1/500 sec. at f/8.

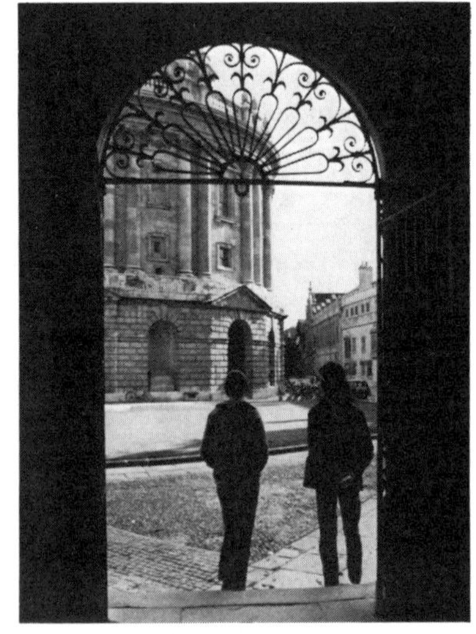

The gateway framing this old building in Oxford makes the scene more appealing. People add scale to the picture. Taken with a 24 mm lens; 1/125 sec. at f/11.

every famous person who ever walked the face of the earth. While most are not worth a second look, now and again you will discover one you really like and absolutely must photograph. The problem is how to make a picture of a statue that isn't just one more dull record shot.

This is Richard the Lion-Hearted, with one of the buildings of Parliament in the background. Sidelighting and careful cropping make this study a good one. Taken with a 50 mm lens; 1/250 sec. at f/11.

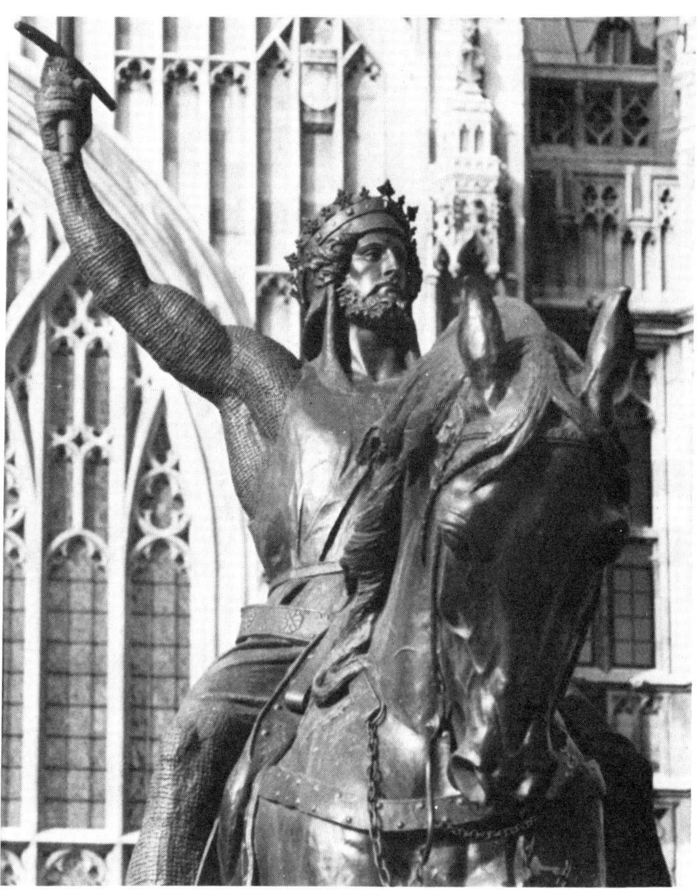

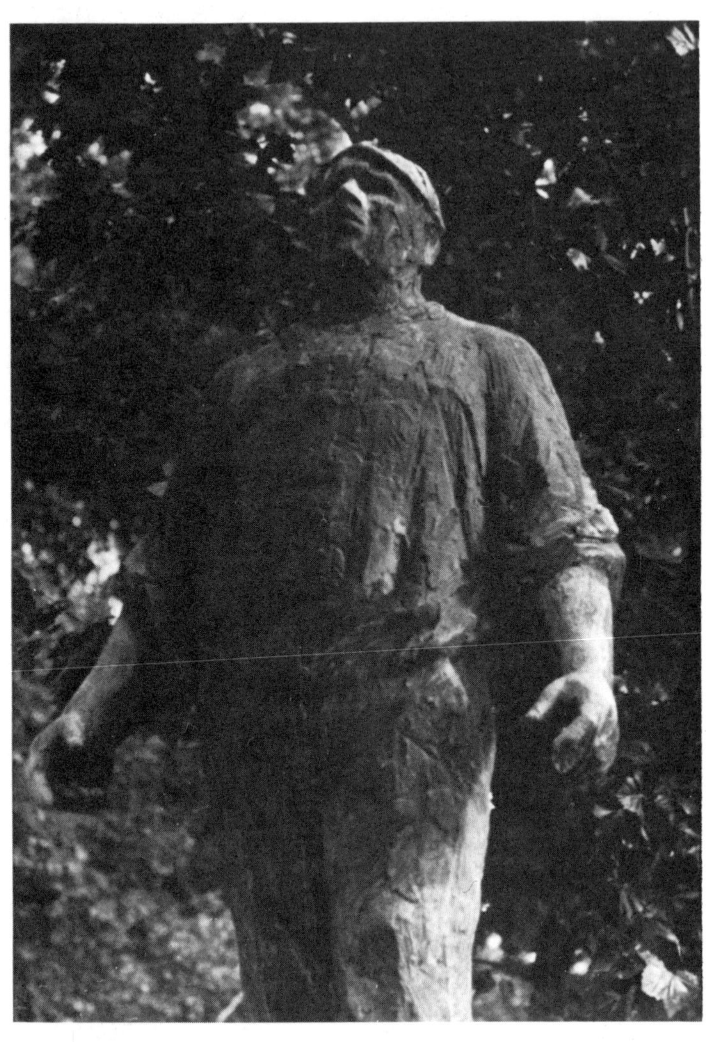

This statue in Amsterdam, "The Dockworker," commemorates the strike against the occupying Nazis in 1941 to protest the deportation of the Jews. The low camera angle makes the figure seem even more powerful. Taken with a 50 mm lens; 1/125 sec. at f/11.

Try a multifaceted prism on the front of your lens to create a multiple image. Or get a real person in the picture with the statue you have selected. If a pigeon wants to land on the statue, shoot it that way. Photograph the statue in the early morning mist, in the rain, or at night with just a touch of moonlight falling on it. Be creative.

Other Structures

Spires. When you are looking for good composition, you will always be glad to find a few sharp vertical lines to

Church spire in Rudesheim, Germany. Out-of-focus branches and leaves hide the bald sky. Taken with a 50 mm lens; 1/60 sec. at f/4, late in the day.

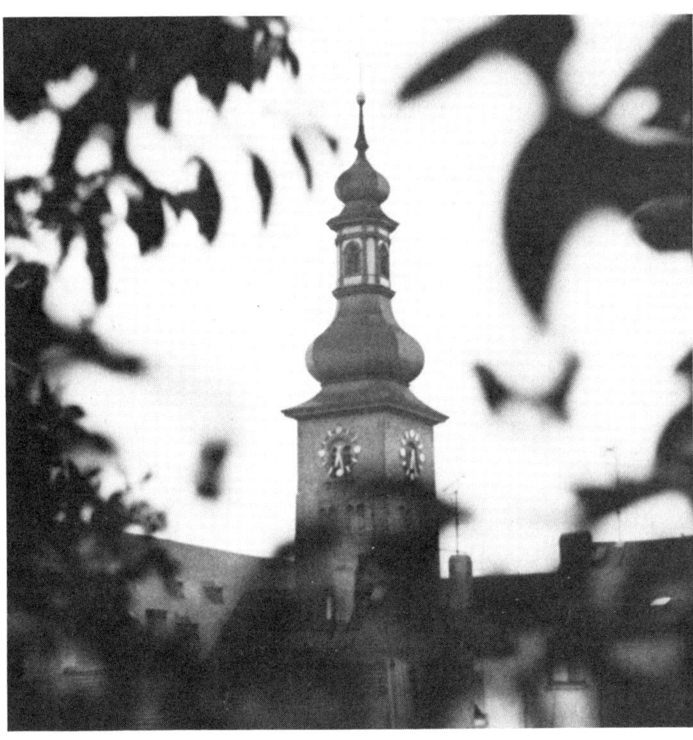

oppose the heavy masses and horizontal shapes in your pictures. Church spires are perfect for this purpose. They come in all shapes and sizes. Some spires are tall and slender, others are short and broad; some are round, or onion-shaped, or square. By themselves, spires are not all that interesting, but when combined with other buildings or included as a part of a landscape, they are very picturesque and beautiful.

In a densely populated city, you may be able to find an area where modern builders still haven't built a forest of unsightly blocks of flats. In such places, you can still make fine panoramas of the old city as it must have looked centuries ago. Such views will be punctuated with a variety of spires that seem to have been carefully located just for you. In the old cathedral cities of Europe, as you approach from the countryside, the first thing you see is the spire of the church. As you move around within the city, every street seems to lead to the cathedral with its lovely, tall spire dominating each urban view.

One day, you will be in just the right place to enjoy a sunset with the spire of a fine old church in silhouette. Be sure to shoot this one in a vertical format so that the spire runs nearly to the top of the picture. What a magazine cover this would make!

Bridges. There are so many different types of bridges throughout the world that you could begin shooting them right now and never run out of bridges to photograph. When you consider the wide variety of bridges you can photograph, you realize that this is a subject which must be a part of your plans. There are little footbridges just wide enough for one person and only long enough for a few steps. At the other end of the spectrum are mile-long bridges that join continents.

Bridges should not be photographed by themselves. But, if you can make a bridge a part of one of your pictures, it will add considerable interest. The Ponte Vecchio in Florence, the center of that city's famous jewelry industry since the Renaissance, has been photographed millions of times. Use the Ponte Vecchio as a backdrop for an interesting scene or event. A few minutes' wait will reward you with such a situation.

Crossing the Peace Bridge in Hiroshima gives one a chilling feeling. The river below was the only refuge on that terrible day in August, 1945.

In the United States, New Englanders are rather proud of their covered bridges.

Some railway bridges are spectacular. They are more than true engineering marvels (which indeed they are); engineers in the days when the railways were built were also artists, who knew how to blend structure with location for a spectacular effect.

Should you happen to see a large drawbridge opening for a small tug while all road traffic is waiting, you might have a picture worth shooting.

Especially interesting are the artistic old bridges built over the industrial canals. Space was provided beneath or over the top for the horses or mules to pass as they pulled barges along the canals. These are lovely old brick structures that make fine photographic subjects.

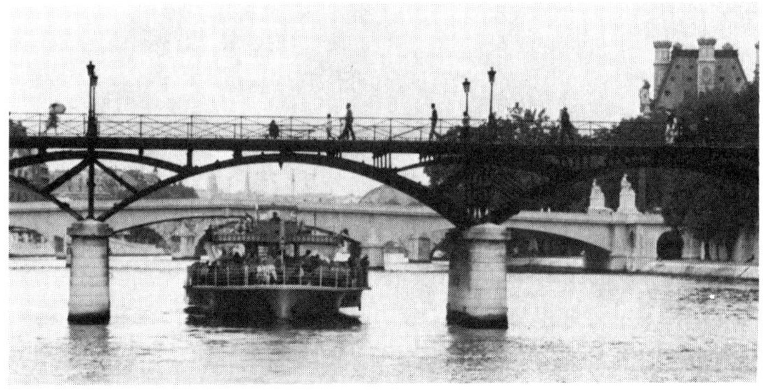

A bâteau-mouche (river sightseeing boat) passes beneath the Pont des Arts in Paris. Taken with a 135 mm lens; 1/500 sec. at f/11.

There are many famous bridges: London Bridge (now in Arizona), Tower Bridge (still in London as of this writing), the bridges over the Seine River in Paris. In the accompanying picture, the Pont des Arts frames a tourist riverboat. This delicate footbridge connects the Louvre and the Palais de l'Institut, seat of the Académie Française. Also spanning the Seine are the ornate Pont Alexandre III and the venerable Pont Neuf, named the "new bridge" in the sixteenth century.

The Charles Bridge in Prague is said to be one of the most beautiful bridges in the world; a photograph of it with the old city behind it could be stunning.

The Rialto, bridging the Grand Canal of Venice, will always make superb picture material. You can photograph it from the canal or on the span itself and it appears to be two different stuctures. There are little shops lining both sides of the Rialto, and when you are on the bridge, you lose all sense of crossing the canal.

Budapest is really two cities—Buda and Pest— divided by the Danube. The river is crossed at many points by fine old bridges.

In Avignon, France, there is a bridge that goes nowhere. French schoolchildren have sung about it for centuries.

The Magdalen Bridge at Oxford in England is backed up by the towers and spires of the great university.

Westminster Bridge in London practically touches the buildings of Parliament. You won't pass any of these calmly by without taking pictures.

Restaurants Inside. If you should come across a restaurant or pub that is really something to rave about, take a picture of it. When you tell people about it later, the photo will help explain what's so exciting.

You don't have to make a big production of it. While you're dining—even in the lowest light level—you can shoot an effective picture. Mount the wide-angle lens on your camera and place the camera on the table beside you. Prefocus and aim by sighting along the line where the lens is pointed. If the camera is near the edge of the table, there won't be a lot of tablecloth at the bottom of your picture. Since the camera is sitting solidly on the table, a long exposure will not be a problem. With the lens wide open, set the shutter for one second and make your exposure. You don't even need to look at the spot where the picture is being taken, if this might alert people in the scene. They'll never know they are being photographed. Since you are not putting your camera up to your eye, most people could be looking right at you and not suspect they are being photographed.

On your way out of the restaurant, you might ask to make a couple of pictures. If the manager turns you down, you still have the pictures you took during the meal. Should you receive permission, use the technique of holding your camera solidly against the rear wall of the room and making a short time exposure.

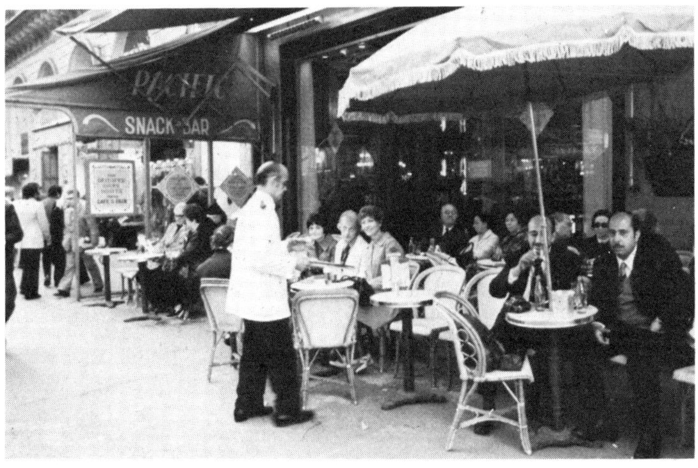

A scene at the famous Café de la Paix, near the Paris Opera, as photographed late in the day. For the low light level, exposure was 1/30 sec. at f/4; taken with a 50 mm lens.

If the manager appears particularly cooperative, ask if you might visit the kitchen for a picture or two. He or she might be delighted to show the place off!

Newsstands. A really good way to add interest to your selection of travel pictures is to seek out those outdoor newsstands where they sell newspapers and magazines. Close-ups of small sections of the display are both colorful and interesting. You might also make a couple of full-frame pictures of individual magazines. Your pictures will show the folks back home what the foreign publications look like and you won't have to haul pounds of magazines to show it. Rather than pictures of only magazines, try to do close-ups of a few front pages of local newspapers. Even if you don't know the language, it is nearly always possible to figure out what the major news stories are through a few key names or words.

Back off now so that the entire newsstand fills your frame, with the man or woman who runs it as your center of interest. He or she will usually cooperate if you're polite and indicate that you are really interested in a good picture.

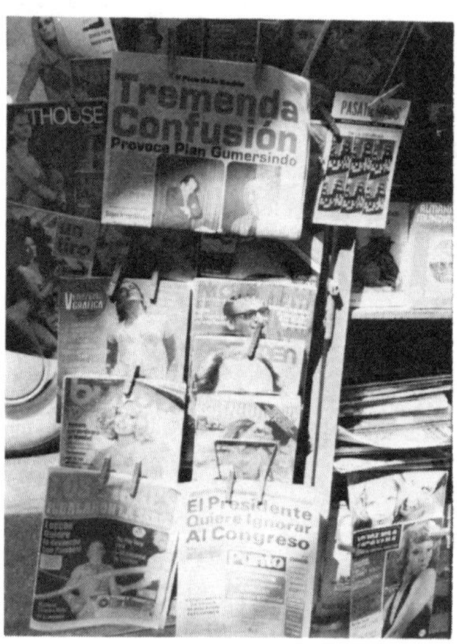

Ideal close-up subjects on your travels are magazine stands that display the local publications. Friends back home can see what they look like without your having to cart tons of them back. Taken with a 50 mm lens; 1/125 sec. at f/11.

SEASCAPES AND HARBORS

What is it about water that excites us all so much? We seem to be drawn to the sea, the seashore, the seaports. Just the word "waterfront" can evoke all sorts of images. It's possible to poke around any waterfront area of one of the world's great cities for days and never shoot the same type of picture twice.

Venice sits there and dares you not to take her picture. She is so easy on the eye (and lens). Whether your favorite Venetian view is looking across the bay to the

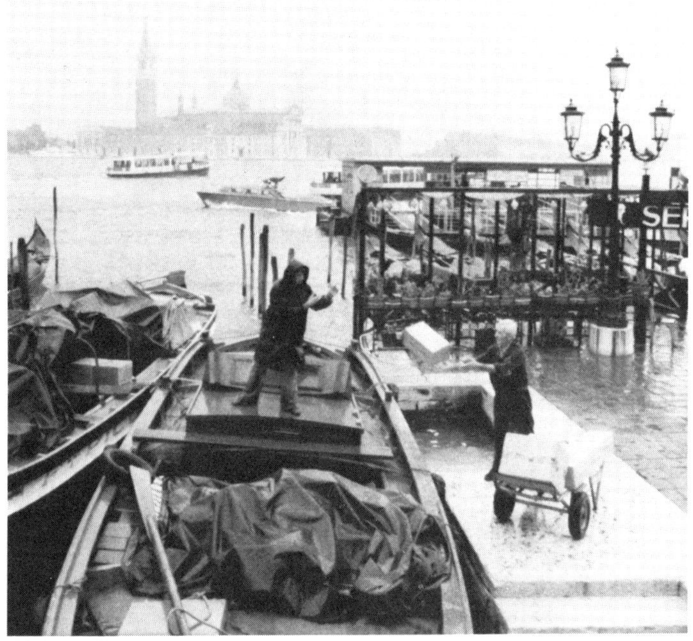

Rain didn't bother these two men unloading a barge in Venice. Although it was carefully planned, the finished picture looks as though it was completely spontaneous. Note the box of goods in mid-air. Taken with a 50 mm lens; 1/125 sec. at f/5.6.

Island of San Giorgio or a general shot of the Grand Canal with the Rialto in the background, the water impressions and reflections are breathtaking. In your excitement, don't forget to carefully calculate your exposure and plan your composition. Treat each picture as though it might be your very best shot.

Did you ever watch the sunrise over one of those picture-book seaports? The mist rises over the water and sea birds turn gracefully in the air above the fishing boats as they set out for the day's catch. This is perfect picture material. Sit on a pier where you can see the harbor, with the fog masking the tops of hills falling steeply into the water. The only sounds you can hear are the breeze, bird calls, and the chug of the fishing boats as they pass in review—especially for you and your camera.

Sunsets are particularly beautiful over harbors. No sunset by itself is unusual until you place an interesting silhouette in front of it. Try a giant windmill on the water-front with a splash of golden-red sunset behind it. Or frame a sunset with that famous London landmark, Tower Bridge.

Closely associated with the harbors and seascapes are the picturesque fish markets. These offer myriad shooting possibilities. Photograph the fishermen with their oilskins, odd-looking hats, and weather-beaten faces.

Do you like to photograph birds? Every waterfront is teeming with birdlife. Seabirds are graceful and make ideal camera subjects. And they'll be around as long as you are willing to click your shutter.

Coiled rope on the weathered dock can make a good close-up shot. Other nautical gear has a flavor all its own. Always consider your backgrounds, so your pictures don't look as if they were taken back home. A little sign—a local sailor, something to identify where your shot was made—will localize your pictures best.

The larger seaports have guided boat tours of their harbors. As you sit on the tour boat, the whole panorama of harbor life passes before your lens. You will see tugs furiously pushing giant liners with seemingly little effort. Busy harbor traffic will show you its best side, from tramp steamers to sleek sailing yachts. Drydocks are interesting, for they show the lower decks of ships, areas that are usually below the surface of the water. Ships with exotic names come from ports all over the world. And don't forget the crews of these foreign ships—more good picture possibilities.

With a little persuasion, you might be able to talk yourself aboard one of the ships in the harbor. Don't be shy; pose the various crew members at the wheel, in the boiler room, and wherever else you think you have a picture. Show them your mini-portfolio and they'll be happy to oblige—if you don't keep them from important work.

Try to meet the harbor police. They could surely tell you a few stories and might suggest a couple of good picture ideas, too. Seek out a fireboat. Firemen are either extremely busy or not busy at all. By introducing yourself, you might find some new friends and a totally different look at the waterfront.

SPECIAL SITUATIONS

Haze and Fog

Some morning on your trip you will get up to find the country wrapped in a thick blanket of fog. Don't go back to bed in disgust. Get out there with your camera and enjoy that fog while it lasts. This may be your chance of a lifetime. Consider yourself most fortunate to be able to shoot under such unusual conditions. Fog can be beautiful if you know how to handle it with your camera.

Work out a plan for the day with this weather condition in mind. In the cities, seek out famous landmarks where you can shoot fog pictures to best advantage.

How about the Town Hall in Stockholm in the foggy background, with a tiny sailboat tied up in the foreground? Or a nearly empty white picture of water and fog with a single Venetian gondola moving across the scene? Standing in St. Mark's Square in Venice in the fog, you see a couple of young lovers walking into the mist, with the Campanile and the Cathedral barely visible in the background. There are many possibilities for using this technique in your pictures.

Haze is not the same as fog, and must be handled differently. Unless you are working on a very clear day, you can expect haze to be present in most pictures. Haze will help you create a third dimension in your otherwise two-dimensional pictures. Consider the mountain photographs you have seen. The nearest mountain is clear and sharp and quite colorful; the mountain behind it is softened by some aerial haze and its color not so vivid; the third mountain back is quite a bit softer and lacking even more in color. Instead of worrying about the fact that there is haze out there, put it to work for you and you'll be glad you did.

Your pictures of old waterfronts will appear much more mysterious when haze is present. Always keep some objects in the foreground which are clear and distinct, and let the haze give the softening effect you are looking for.

Night Pictures

Some night pictures should be in your collection from your trip. These are not difficult to do and the contrast with your regular daytime shots will be spectacular. The famous shopping streets of the world are brightly lighted and can be photographed with a hand-held camera. You will surely want to make a couple of pictures of all those brightly colored signs and the lights of the automobiles.

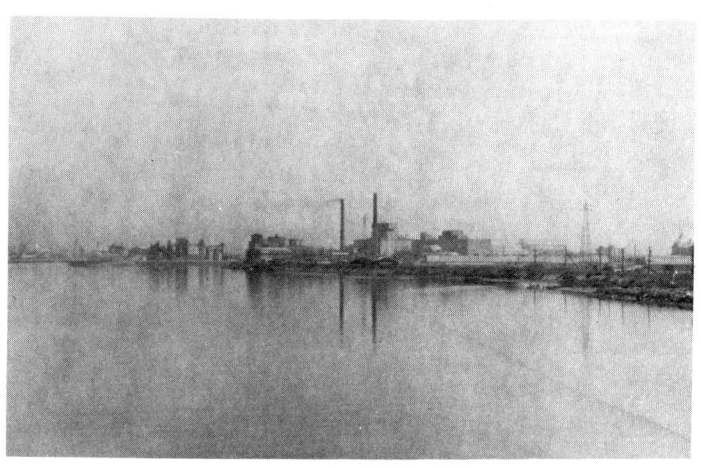

This industrial view was made from a train window in Japan. The entire scene is greatly lightened by haze, but the resulting high-key picture looks much like an etching. Taken with a 50 mm lens; 1/500 sec. at f/4.

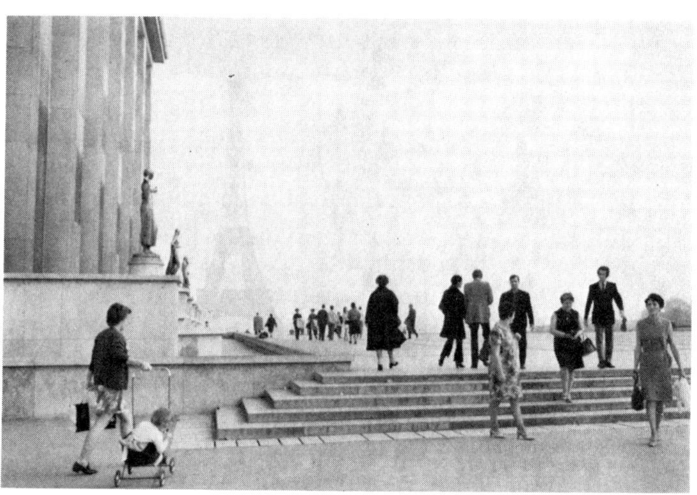

When you encounter haze, use it to your advantage. In a picture like this, make sure you have people or some other objects in the foreground. Taken with a 24 mm lens; 1/250 sec. at f/11.

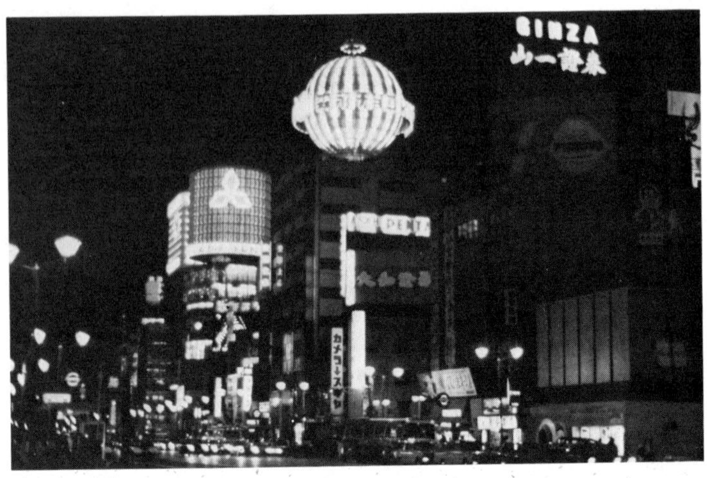

A night picture like this of the Tokyo Ginza district is easy to shoot. The bright illumination allows rather short, hand-held exposures. This picture was made with a 50 mm lens; 1/30 sec. at f/1.4. It is wise to make several slightly different night exposures and then select the best.

A minimum of special equipment for night pictures will assure good results. A small tripod and a cable release are all you really need. If you are shooting color film, a conversion filter such as the Kodak 80B filter will change the color balance of the lighting to match your daylight-type film. While it is possible to shoot hand-held pictures at night with your lens wide open, better quality is obtained with a tripod-mounted camera; stop your lens down a couple of *f*-stops and slow your shutter accordingly.

When you meter for night pictures, point your meter slightly downward so it isn't sensing the brightest area of the scene. Calculate your exposure at that brightness level. If you are using the 80B conversion filter, remember that it requires an exposure factor. You must make a longer exposure than usual because the filter absorbs quite a bit of light—probably making a difference of a couple of *f*-stops.

The best time to make night pictures is not at night. If you can time things just right, make these shots either just before sunset or just after dawn. Lights will be burning brightly—especially just before sunset—but your pictures will show detail in those areas that would normally show nothing but black in true night pictures.

Consider a view of a shopping street at twilight where none of the lights are turned on. You can see everything in detail—the sky is a dark blue, all the buildings are a blueish color, and you can see all the people. Now turn on all the lights and the colored signs. The effect is a night-time scene, but you can see everything—not just the lights. The picture of the Cologne street in the color section was shot at this time of evening. Basically, the extra lighting was used to fill the shadow areas. The imbalance of color between the natural twilight and the artificial lighting is quite dramatic.

Rain Pictures

Don't let a little rain stop you from shooting pictures. If you do, you will be missing a lot. You can get some of your best pictures if you will take the initiative and work with your camera in the rain.

Unless it's really pouring, you can work rather easily with your camera in the rain. All you need in special equipment is a small umbrella, one that folds into a short, easy-to-carry size. By making a simple hook, you can carry it on your belt or hooked onto a shoulder bag on days when you think you may need it. You might want to lighten your load further by carrying less film than you would usually take; also, you will use your telephoto lens a lot less—if at all.

Changing lenses in the rain is not the same as on clear days. You always risk getting a few raindrops on the front or rear surfaces of your lenses—or even inside your camera on the mirror. While this moisture will not cause permanent damage, until those little droplets are gone you

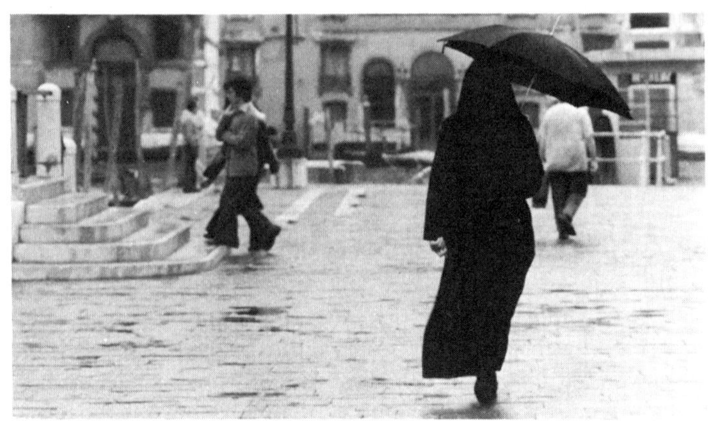

Pictures in the rain can be very effective. Always look for a specific center of interest—in this case, the nun with the umbrella. When the background is just right, shoot. Taken in Venice with a 50 mm lens; 1/125 sec. at f/5.6.

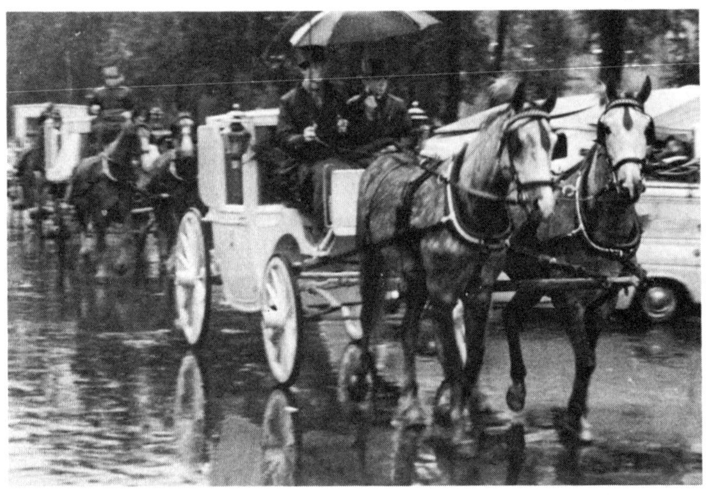

Amsterdam is where the photographer found these horse-drawn carriages in the pouring rain. The effect is better than if the sun had been shining. The camera was ready to shoot when they appeared on the scene; exposure was 1/125 sec. at f/4 with a 50 mm lens.

will not get the best quality images. Keep a clean, dry handkerchief available for such problems. You don't want to quit shooting because of a few drops of rain on a lens. To keep your equipment as dry as possible, duck into a doorway to change your lenses. Keep your camera protected with one side of your raincoat, or at least with a lenshood or a lenscap. Even your hand cupped over the lens will protect it nicely.

This extra effort is definitely worth it. Shooting in the rain lends itself to the truly artistic flair. Reflections add much to a scene that would otherwise be dull. A puddle of rainwater with drops falling into it and colored lights reflecting on its surface can become a thing of lovely, abstract beauty.

The white sky of a rainy day is not particularly attractive or interesting. In general, try to compose your pictures so that little or no sky is in the scene. This is rarely a problem when you're shooting within a city, as you are often surrounded by buildings. Sometimes, you can back into a doorway to frame your picture, keep the rain off your camera, and block out that nasty white sky! On the other hand, the lighting is easiest to control under cloudy skies, because there are no deep, harsh shadows.

Out in the country, you will have a little more trouble eliminating the white sky. If this proves to be the case, turn the tables and feature it as the dominating part of your picture. Perhaps you have spotted a lonely shepherd, sitting on a hill looking after his flock. By positioning him near the bottom of the picture with a large expanse of white sky above him, you can lend the feeling of dreary weather that just fits the mood you are hoping to create.

While we're on the subject of large areas of white sky, let's go into it a bit more. Rain or no rain, there are many situations where the bright sky in the background of your pictures is the brightest area in the scene. This is quite distracting and you should try to work around it. As you look through your proof sheets, you will note that more pictures than you would like to admit have this common fault. By moving around a little closer, a little to the left, a little to the right, you could have blocked that white area out completely. The main center of interest should be the easiest area to find in the picture. Look at a copy of *National Geographic* or any other magazine noted for its fine scenic photography, and see how many of the great pictures in there have large patches of white in the background. Not many, we'd guess—if any!

Try a portrait in the rain where your subject has little droplets of water on his or her face. You'll notice that under this kind of lighting there is a main direction of light, but all shadows are nicely filled and there are no harsh deep shadows in the eyes and under the nose. This diffuse light is extremely flattering. Also, for some reason, in the rain, colors seem to be soft and subtle, yet quite intense.

If you must slow down your shutter because the light isn't as bright as you are used to having it, don't worry about it. Some of your pictures made this way might show a little movement. This suggestion of motion will make your shots that much more charming.

Interiors

Don't forget that interiors are just as important as exteriors. Even without tripods or flash, today's fast films make it possible to photograph under almost any lighting conditions, and time exposures will always be possible.

If you have never photographed interiors before, a rainy day is a good time to start, since you will almost certainly be indoors anyway. Shooting interiors is no more difficult than working outside. Since the color of the lighting is slightly different than daylight, you should use tungsten-type film, but all the other rules hold true. You don't need a tripod, either. There is usually plenty of light. Museums in many foreign countries will not allow tripods or flash. This will rarely be an insurmountable problem.

Some public buildings allow no cameras at all. If you know this in advance, leave your camera in the hotel.

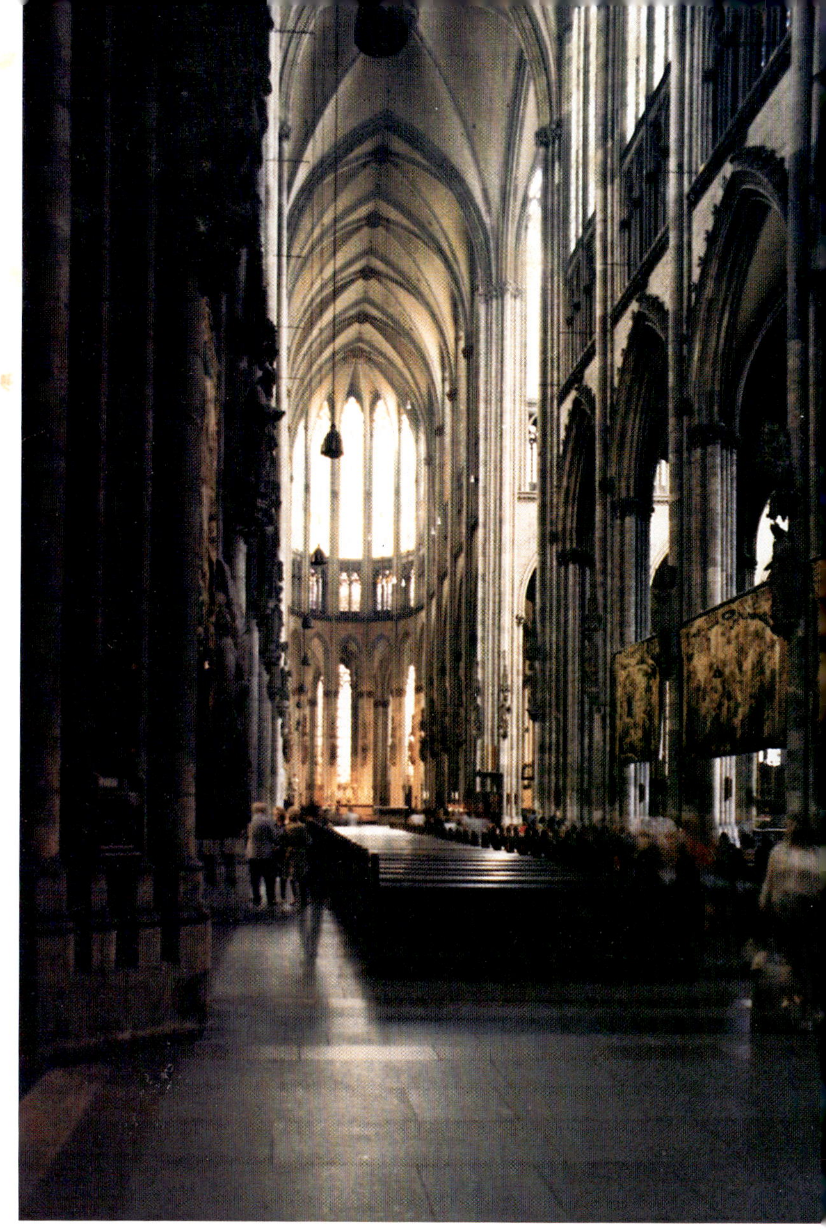

For this interior shot of Cologne Cathedral, the camera was rested on a table and held in position while a 1-sec. exposure was made. Since the back of the camera was held in a perfectly vertical position, vertical lines in the finished picture are truly parallel. Some of the foreground was cropped when the finished print was made. Taken with a 24 mm lens; 1 sec. at f/8.

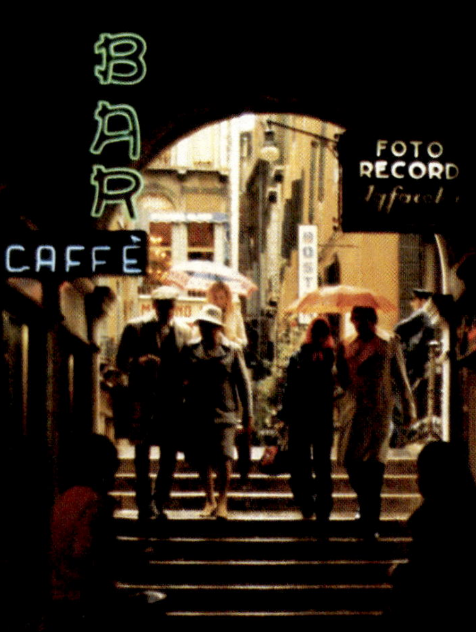

BAR
A
CAFFÈ
FOTO
RECORD
KODACHROME

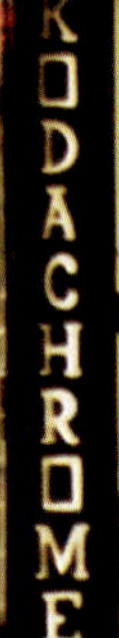

At left: When it rains, the wet pavement gives off reflections that really add to color pictures. This interesting interior was shot in Venice in one of the galleries just off St. Mark's Square. Taken with a 24 mm lens; 1/30 sec. at f/4.

Below: Looe, an English Channel port near Plymouth. The photographer's host, who drove him to this lovely little village, was most apologetic about the fog: it was impossible to see the tops of the hills surrounding the harbor. In fact, it could not have been more beautiful—just right for pictures. Taken with a 50 mm lens; 1/125 sec. at f/16.

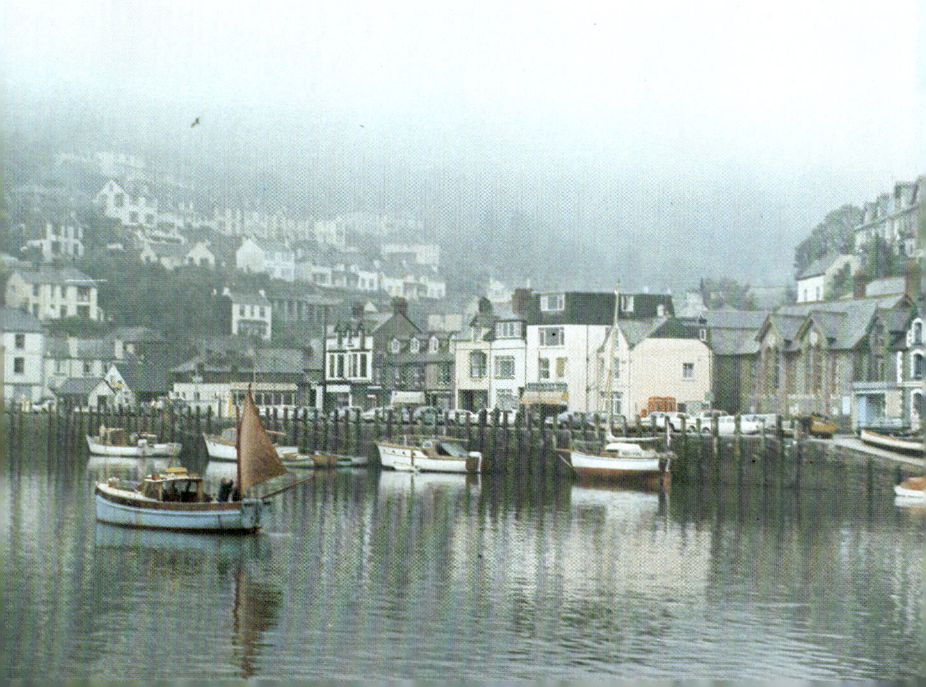

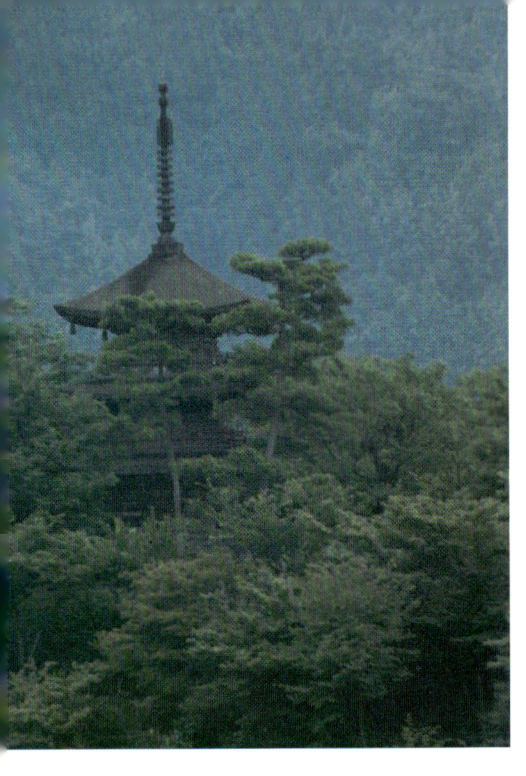

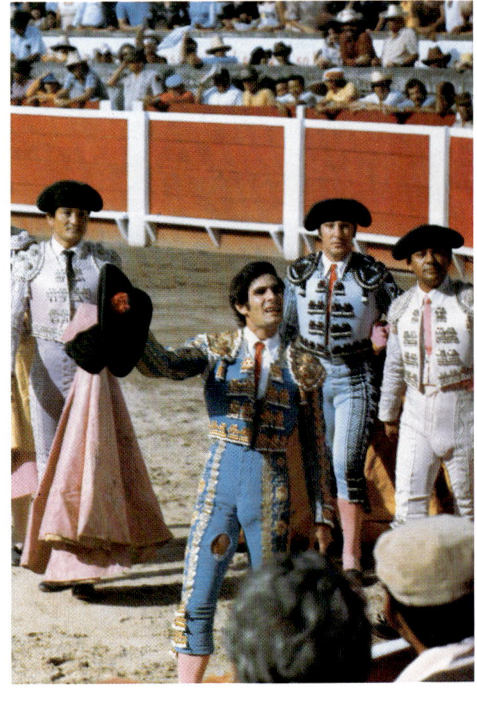

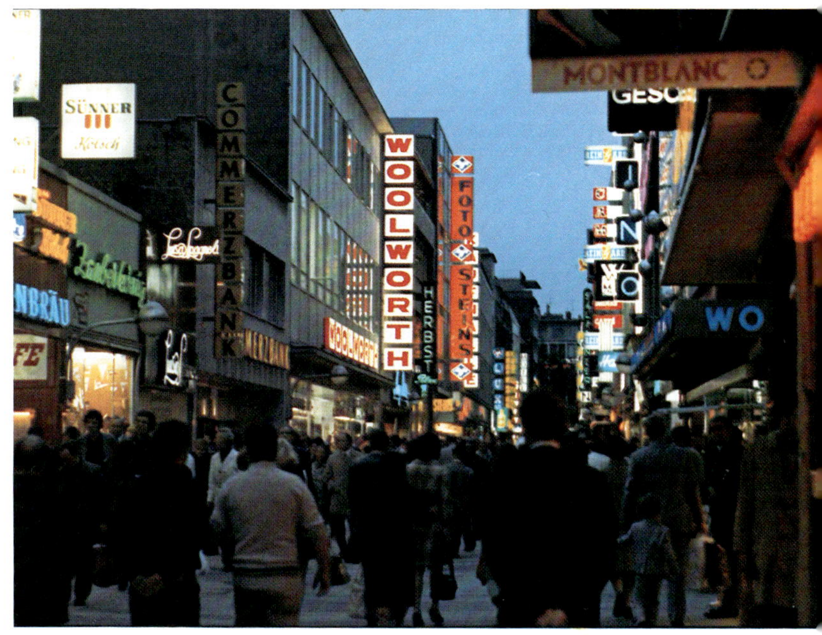

Above: Hohestrasse, a shopping street in Cologne, Germany. This picture was made just before dark to allow the best combination of available light from the signs and the twilight sky. Taken with a 50 mm lens; 1/15 sec. at f/2.8.

Opposite page, top: The Japanese are renowned for their ability to blend their architecture with nature. This beautiful temple is situated in the hills north of Kyoto. Taken with a 135 mm lens; 1/250 sec. at f/5.6.

Below left: A Spanish matador accepts the acclaim of the crowd after killing his bull and being awarded the ears. Apparently the bull did not give up without leaving his own mark on the matador. Taken with a 135 mm lens; 1/250 sec. at f/16.

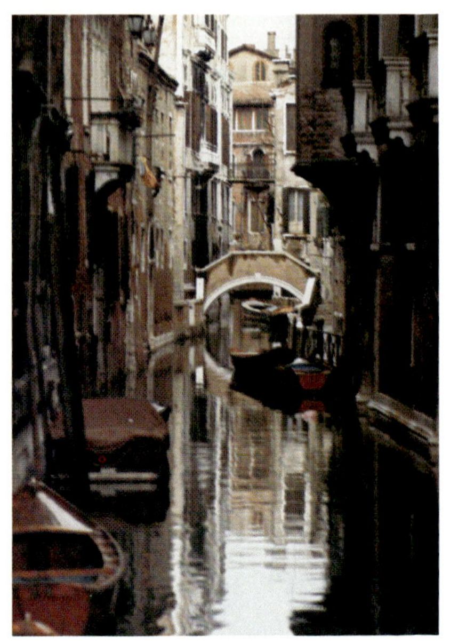

In Venice it seems impossible to point one's camera in a wrong direction. This is just one of many beautiful canal scenes. Taken with a 50 mm lens; 1/125 sec. at f/11.

Here is one of the most beautiful scenes in all of England, or perhaps the world. This is Thomas Hardy country—Shaftesbury in Dorset, with the Vale of Blackmore in the background. Taken with a 50 mm lens; 1/125 sec. at f/11.

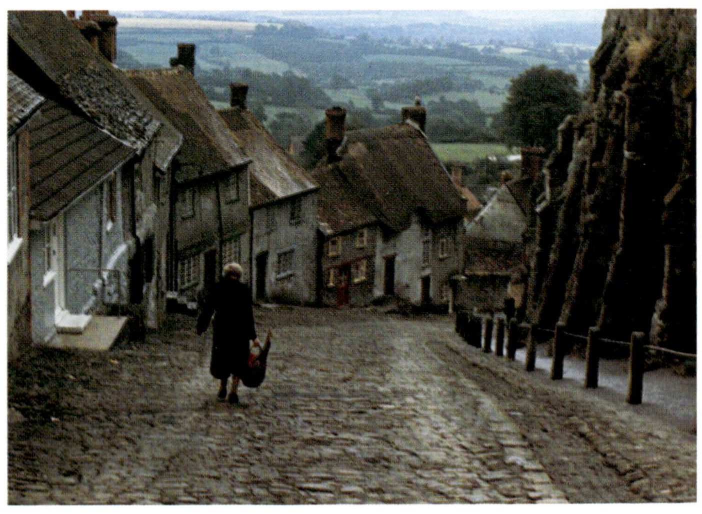

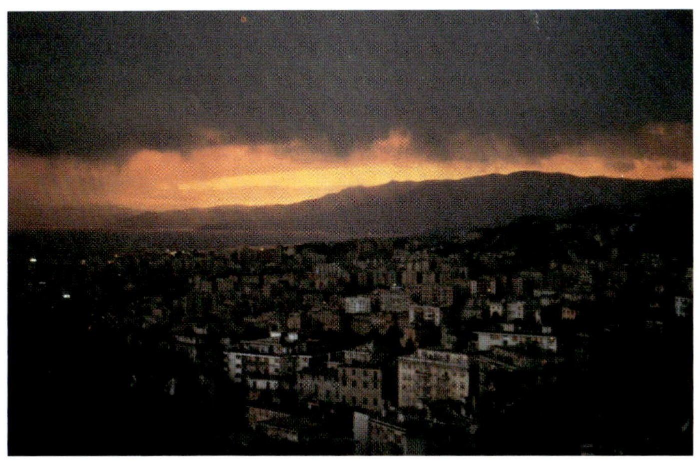

A storm is brewing over the Mediterranean near Genoa, Italy. Taken with a 50 mm lens; 1/30 sec. at f/1.4.

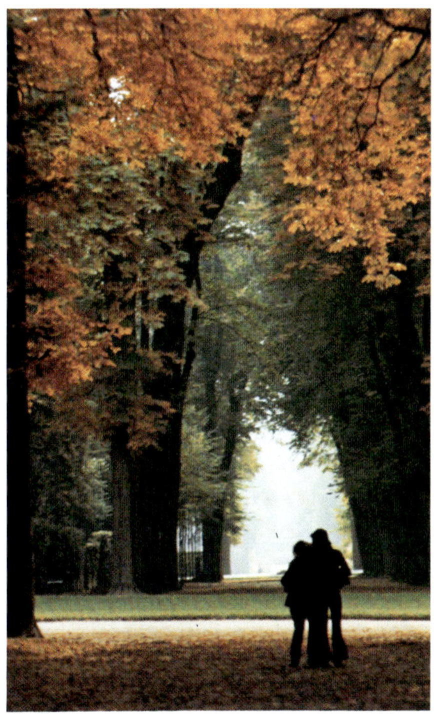

Lovers in the seemingly endless grounds of the Palace of Versailles. Trees in the background suggest a cathedral interior. Taken with a 135 mm lens; 1/125 sec. at f/5.6.

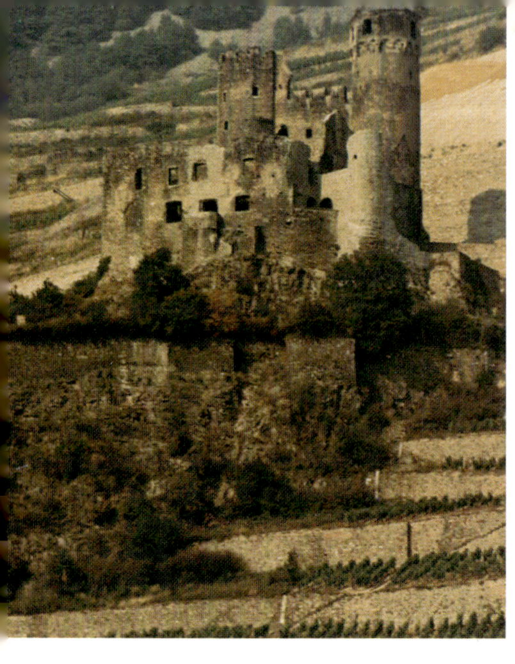

The ruins of the old castle of Ehrenfels, set on a vineyard-covered slope above the Rhine River in Germany, seems almost part of the natural landscape. Taken from a moving riverboat with a 135 mm lens; 1/250 sec. at f/8.

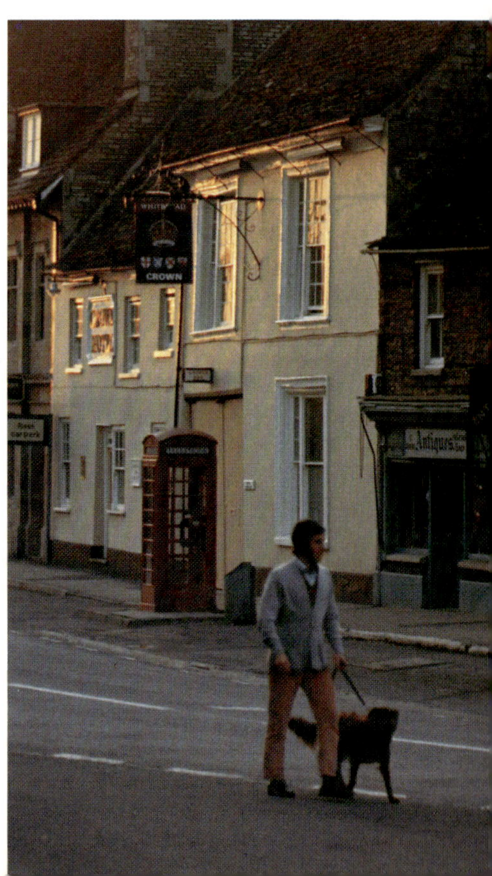

In this picture, taken at sunset, the only indications of the sun itself are the golden reflections in the windows of an English "pub." The man and his dog aid composition. Taken with a 50 mm lens; 1/125 sec. at f/4.

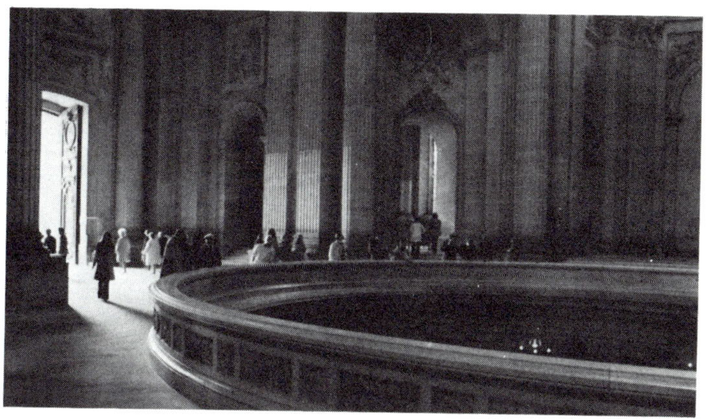

*Inside the Invalides is the tomb of Napoleon. This view
shows the circular opening beneath the dome of the building.
In the crypt below is the Emperor's marble sarcophagus. A
slow shutter speed (1/60 sec.) and a wide aperture (f/5.6.)
permitted this hand-held photograph by available light,
taken with a 24 mm lens.*

Checking it at the reception desk of a museum or other
public building makes some people nervous, so try to find
out in advance what the camera policy is.

The wide-angle lens is ideal for interiors. This lens
will serve you well in two ways: by offering great depth of
field, and by engaging you to encompass a much larger
area in your pictures than you would with your normal
lens.

Remember, as discussed earlier, to keep the back of
your camera truly vertical, so that the vertical lines in your
interior pictures are not distorted. It's easier to do it in the
camera than to correct in the darkroom.

When metering interior pictures, be sure your meter
is not fooled by the bright light coming through a window
into the scene. Even if you plan to include this window in
the picture, do your metering away from it. If your camera
is automatic, bypass the automation if possible. Remember, though, if you take your automatic camera into the

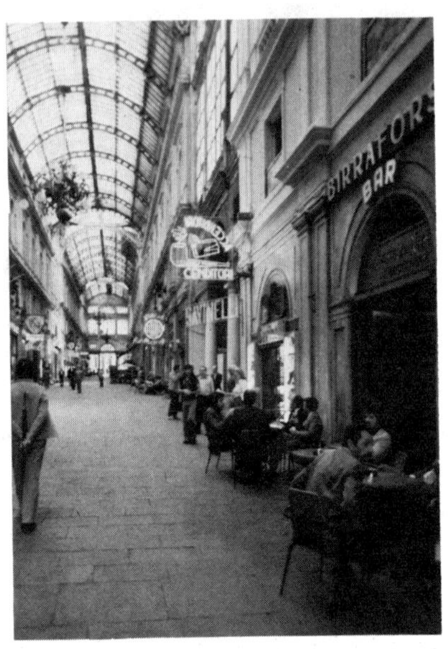

An interior shot of one of the many skylighted galleries in Genoa, Italy, where shoppers and strollers may take coffee without going outdoors, was taken with a 24 mm lens, 1/125 sec. at f/11.

manual mode, to restore the automation when you are finished so you don't spend the rest of the day shooting at the wrong aperture.

Interiors need not necessarily be public buildings. If you are invited to visit the homes of new friends, don't neglect to photograph these interiors as well. Be sure to include the people who live there. They will be pleased to cooperate and your pictures will be that much more interesting. You might offer to send them a slide or print after you return home, but don't make promises for more pictures than you can deliver. In fact, rather than have a picture of their own home, your friends might prefer to have a picture of yours.

Aerials

Pictures taken from the air are always interesting. If you can work it out, make at least a few aerials while you're on your trip.

The easiest—and least expensive—way to make aerials is to shoot from your jetliner. It can be done if you know the basic rules. First, you must have a window seat, which you should request when seats are being assigned at the terminal. Early arrivals have the best seat selection. Tell the agent at the check-in counter what you want to do. Also, be certain your window seat is not over the wing, which would effectively block any view of the ground. The best place from which to shoot is ahead of the wing. The hot engines (if they're mounted under the wings) produce quite a bit of distortion for pictures if you're seated behind the wing. Some jets have the engines mounted on the sides and rear of the body of the plane, and this would not be a problem then.

A second consideration is the direction of your flight and the time of day. If you're flying from south to north in the morning, the sun would be on your right side, so ask for a left window seat.

Although you will look out your window from 39,000 feet up in the air and marvel over the beautiful view (providing there are few clouds), forget about shooting pictures of the ground. There will always be so much aerial haze that your pictures will be a solid blue color. No filter will remove this much haze. You may, however, get some beautiful shots of cloud banks, if the weather conditions are right. While there may be a heavy overcast on the ground, you will probably fly above it. Especially at sunrise and sunset, the colors of the sky and of the clouds below you are breathtaking.

The only way to get good aerial shots of the ground is to shoot only when the plane is near the ground—and then, almost only on landing. On take-off, you will get very little, as the plane climbs quite rapidly and you will have great difficulty making any decent pictures. However, as the plane is in the landing pattern, you can expect to get quite a few different shots before touching down.

With a little practice, you will bring home some interesting shots of the countryside. Unfortunately, you can't expect to shoot aerials of the city centers, as your plane is not likely to have a glidepath that runs over the city. (The exception to this might be if the plane is ordered into a holding pattern because of some delay on the ground. The holding pattern might be directly over the city.) In any event, there are still some good pictures to be had if you keep your eyes open.

Always be on the lookout for a center of interest for your aerial pictures. A little village like the one in the accompanying photograph is an example, for it directs the eye's attention to itself. Too many pictures taken from the air are views rather than pictures: nothing happens. Consider a center of interest each time you're ready to snap a picture from the air.

Should you want to do aerial photography extensively, there are ways to do it. When you inquire about hiring a plane and pilot, you will discover that it is expensive. Also, you will have to declare what you intend to

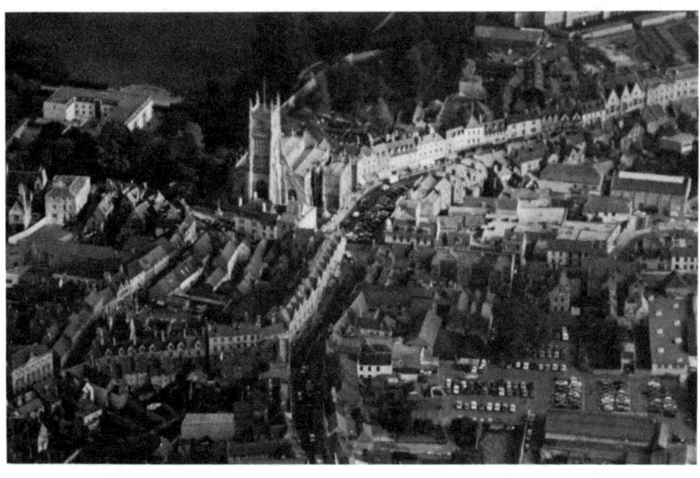

In this aerial photograph of Cirencester in England's Cotswold Hills, note that the parish church provides a focal point. Too many aerials lack such a center of interest and so are rather uninteresting. Taken with a 50 mm lens; 1/500 sec. at f/11.

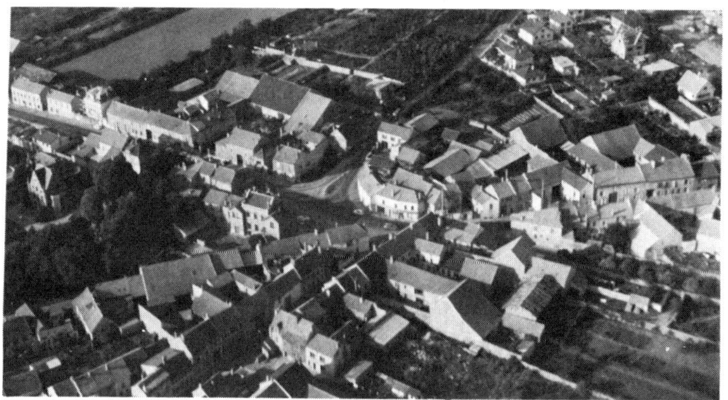

This photograph was made from a jetliner approaching Orly airport at Paris. Pictures such as this must be made during landings, as planes rise too quickly on takeoff for picture opportunities. Always look for a scene with a center of interest—in this case, the intersection of roads creating the pattern of rooflines. Taken with a 50 mm lens; 1/1000 sec. at f/5.6.

photograph, and the plane owner is required by law in most countries to fly only after you have received a government permit. This usually involves considerable red tape and possibly a certain amount of bribery. Unless you're going to make a major commercial effort in this direction, forget it. A series of letters before you leave home might assure you of the proper credentials for each of the countries in which you wish to shoot aerials. Such pictures would probably be good, but remember that they will be only a small part of what you will be photographing on your trip. For the effort and money expended, you might wonder if it's worth it.

There is an alternative. Go to the civilian airfield nearest where you want to shoot aerials. Seek out the local flying club and ask if it is possible to join the club for a day. This is often quite possible. You will be made a member for a nominal charge and one of the club members will be assigned to take you for a tour by air of the sights you would like to see—and photograph. You'll most likely be in a small, single-engine plane. If you want to take pictures, they will probably open a window or remove a door from the light plane for your convenience. It's all quite unofficial, but it works. Since the pilot must have the proper license to take you up as a passenger, you know he's competent.

By instructing your pilot to fly at the minimum altitude, which is usually 800 to 1,000 feet (244 to 305 metres), you can shoot pictures to your heart's content. Since you are now shooting directly, rather than through a plastic window, your resolution will be better than in a larger plane.

Before you leave on your trip, get a map of the area where you want to fly and mark it with brightly colored brush pen. Then discuss it with your pilot. He'll offer his comments and suggestions, and tell you whether some areas are out-of-bounds—for example, the glidepath of the big jets landing nearby. Also make sure you and your pilot understand each other completely—a language barrier can create considerable problems.

Take plenty of film with you for your flight, because you will be surprised at the number of different subjects that will appear before your lens once you become airborne.

If you're shooting slide film, it is important to place a haze filter over your lens, because there will be haze to contend with even though you intend to work rather close to the ground. This is especially true whenever you shoot off to the horizon, for you will be looking across a great distance. Haze is less of a problem with color negative film, as you can make this slight color adjustment in the printing process.

There seems to be a difference of opinion as to which lens is best for aerials. Some prefer the normal lens; others like a slightly longer lens, such as the 85 mm or 100 mm. If you are limited in your kit, stay with your 50 mm normal lens. Your resolution will be best with the 50 mm, and this is an important consideration, as your pictures will hold small details requiring close examination.

If possible, try an aerial photographic excursion at home to check everything out. Shoot a few aerials of town, one or two of which can go in your pocket portfolio. This could be a sort of dress rehearsal flight, where you can check out your equipment and exposure. Then, when you are doing it for your trip, you will know what to expect.

Stage Pictures

If you are planning to attend any theatrical productions, be prepared to shoot at least some pictures of stage action.

If you will be shooting in color, it is imperative that you have some indoor- or tungsten-type film with you. Were you to use regular daylight-type color film with a conversion filter, the exposure factor of that filter would reduce your light to the point of impracticality.

You may prefer this alternative to tungsten-type film: high-speed daylight film and an 80B conversion filter. This would give you a converted film which is essentially the same speed as your regular normal-speed daylight film. If you are shooting color negative film, this is the only alternative, as there is no regular tungsten-type negative film available except in long rolls of at least 100-foot (30.5 m) lengths which you must load yourself.

When shooting pictures in the theatre, you must consider the other people around you. If your camera shutter noise disturbs them at all, you should stop at once. Shoot only during peaks of sound, as when the chorus is trying to outsing the orchestra or during applause or laughter. Even during dramatic productions, there may be times when you can trip your shutter when nobody will hear you—not even the person sitting next to you or in front of you.

Upon entering the theatre, don't brandish your camera. Have it carefully put away—with lens removed, if possible. Some theatres have definite rules against cameras and you might have to check yours at the door.

Never expect to shoot flash or strobe in any theatre. Not only would you disturb your neighbors, you would also annoy the performers on stage. They are there for your entertainment, but not for that sort of distraction. Tripods are also out, for similar reasons. You must work with your hand-held camera, and as quietly as possible.

Since you're going to be working with a hand-held camera and under rather low-level lighting conditions, you should use a normal or only a very short telephoto lens—nothing longer than you can hold with ease. There is an old rule of thumb which might apply here: The longest focal length lens you should use should be the reciprocal of the shortest possible shutter speed called for. For example, at a given *f*-stop, you find that you can shoot at 1/125 sec. Then the longest focal length lens you should consider hand-holding would be a 125 mm lens. If you have a 135 mm lens with you, you could probably stretch a point and use it. On the other hand, your normal 50 mm lens will allow you a higher shutter speed at a larger aperture.

Sports

Sports are a national pastime the world over. Some may be unfamiliar, but most are enjoyable. Of course, they also make superb photo subjects.

In Venezuela, a popular sport is *coleo* (Spanish for "tail twist"). Played on horseback, the object is to grasp a bull by the tail and twist it until the bull is on his back. The rider who accomplishes this feat in the shortest amount of time wins. A participation sport, the only equipment needed are horse, saddle, leather gloves—and nerve.

The most popular sport in the world today is football (pronounced futeball). In the United States it is called soccer. Call it what you like, when two top football teams meet, it's bedlam! Not all of the action is on the field. A ticket to one of these games is not expensive, and if you have a couple of long lenses, a number of good action

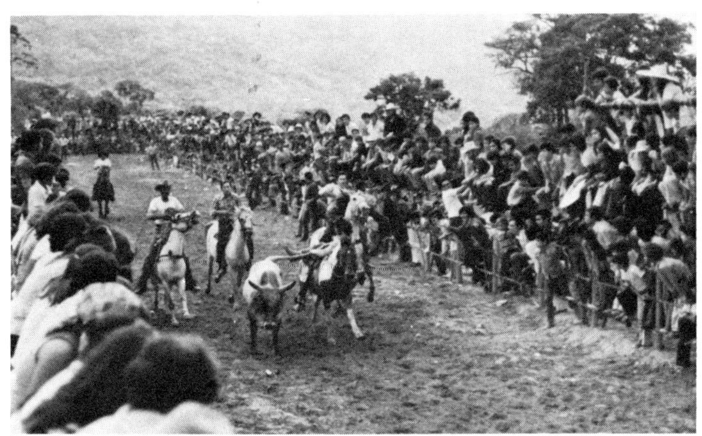

This rodeo in Venezuela must be seen to be appreciated. Called the coleo *(tail twist), the rider must grab the tail of the bull and twist until the bull has been turned on his back. The setting is perfect—no signs or telephone poles to distract. Taken with a 50 mm lens; 1/1000 sec. at f/5.6.*

pictures should result. Try to get pictures of the fans, too, as they really become involved in the game.

Whatever your opinion of its morality or cruelty, you cannot deny that the pageantry of the bullring is unsurpassed. If you've never attended a bullfight, please reserve your judgment until after you have seen one. Although this is a tradition that goes back more years than anyone can count, never was there a single sport that seems better designed for the camera—especially the most sophisticated ones with automatic exposure metering and motor drive. The *corrida* has color, action, and savagery. To see it, all you need is a ticket and a bagful of film. From the opening trumpet to the last bull, when the matador is carried out of the ring on the shoulders of his *aficionados*, there is something to photograph.

Be sure to read up on bullfighting before you visit one of the countries where you can attend. Some knowledge of the sport is essential for you to really understand what you are seeing and shooting. The ability to distin-

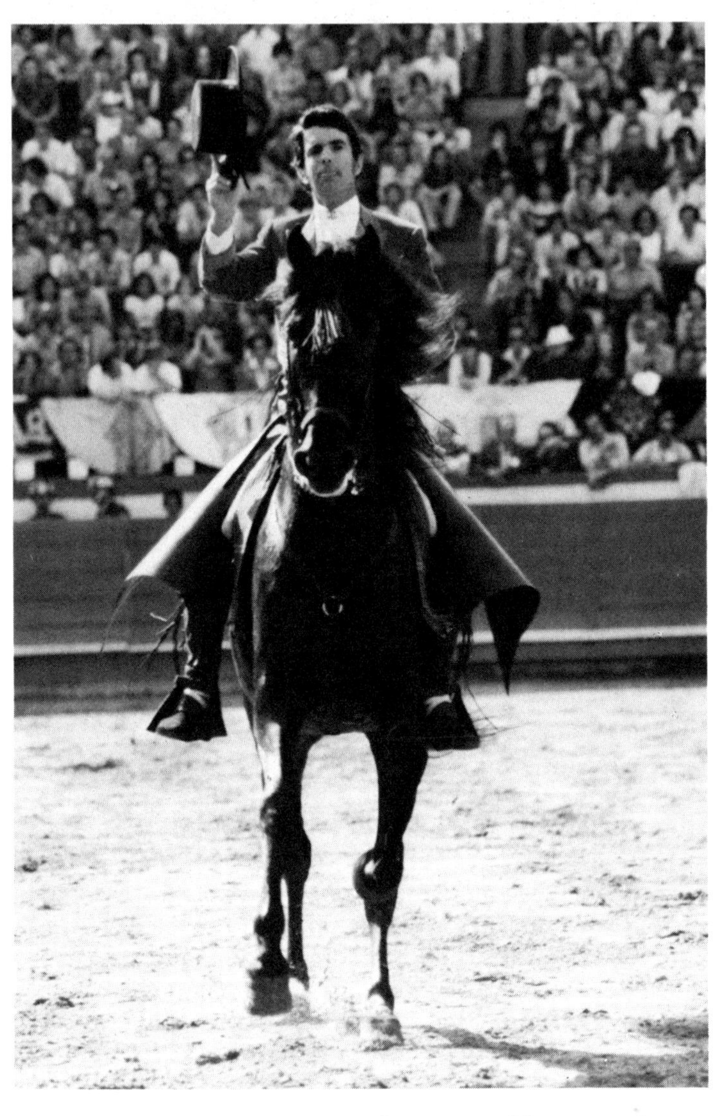

In Portugal, bullfighting is done on horseback. Both rider and horse are to be commended. Taken with a 135 mm lens; 1/1000 sec. at f/5.6.

guish a good pass from a bad one will make the difference between a good picture and a poor one.

MISCELLANEOUS

Trains

If you're a train buff, you'll probably want to spend some extra time in the railway stations of the cities you visit. Aside from the trains themselves, both old and shiny new, many other photo opportunities will present themselves: other travelers, railway employees, signs, signals, posters, the architecture of the stations are just a few possibilities.

On at least one stop on your trip, you may discover an obscure little railway. By all means abandon your previously arranged schedule and have a fling on the train. You'll be pleased that you took the initiative. For example, there is a narrow-gauge line running from Genoa, away from the sea into the mountains to a little town called Casella, a distance of about 25 kilometres. The trip is an absolute gem. The train is electric and very old but well maintained, exactly resembling the type of train set children used to get for Christmas before the streamlined ones came along. The people on board will make great picture subjects.

As the train makes a round trip in a few hours and an excursion ticket, including lunch at the local restaurant, is very inexpensive, this trip is tailor-made for a quick camera outing. The mountain scenery is breathtaking. This is not so much a trip from Genoa to Casella as a rural trip through Italy in general. There are vineyards on the mountainsides, lovely old groups of farm buildings, and the local church—all placed as though an art director had been there and specified where each tree, building, or farm should be placed. The track crews still work with muscle rather than machines.

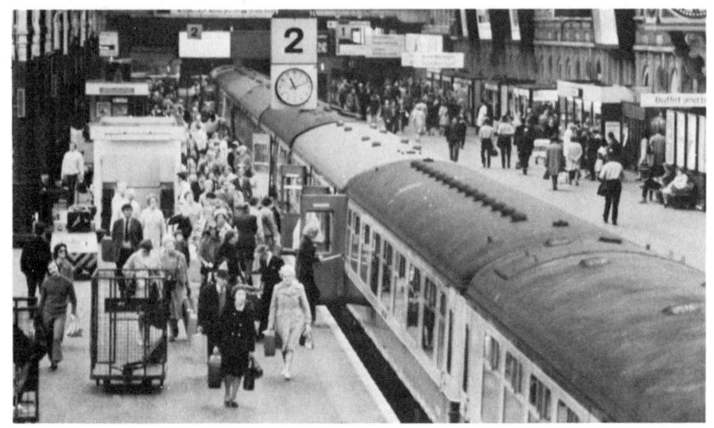

Paddington Station in London, when a train arrives, is a fascinating place to be with your camera. There are all sorts of people worth photographing. Taken with a 135 mm lens; 1/125 sec. at f/3.2.

Casella is a sleepy little hill town. Few automobiles are to be seen. The only action to be seen in town will probably be a quiet game of bowls played by a few men in the churchyard.

When shooting train pictures, be sure to move in for close-up shots of all the little details that make railroading such an interesting subject. Signaling equipment, brass fittings on the engines, wheels, smoke and steam, time-tables, tickets—all are features your camera will just love.

This lovely view was photographed during the narrow-gauge train ride from Genoa to Casella, Italy, described in the text. A 135 mm lens was used, and since the photo was made from a train, the fastest possible shutter speed was used: 1/1000 sec. at f/4. Because the train window was open, there were no problems of reflection or distortion.

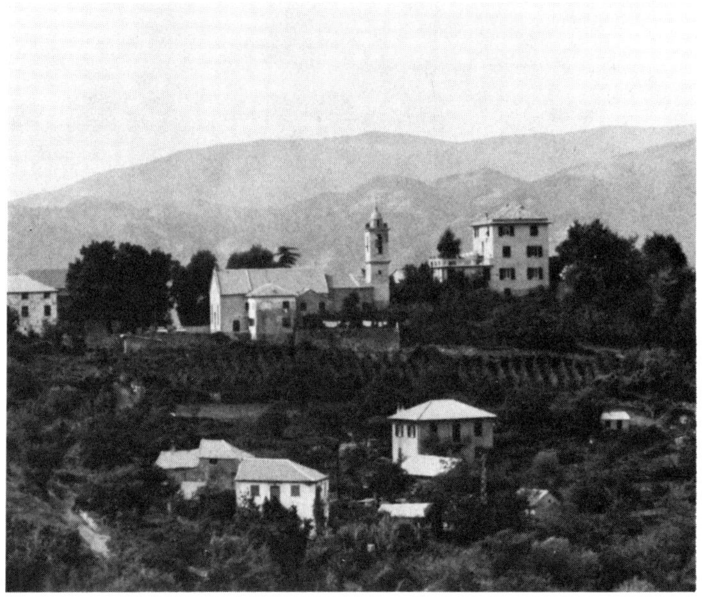

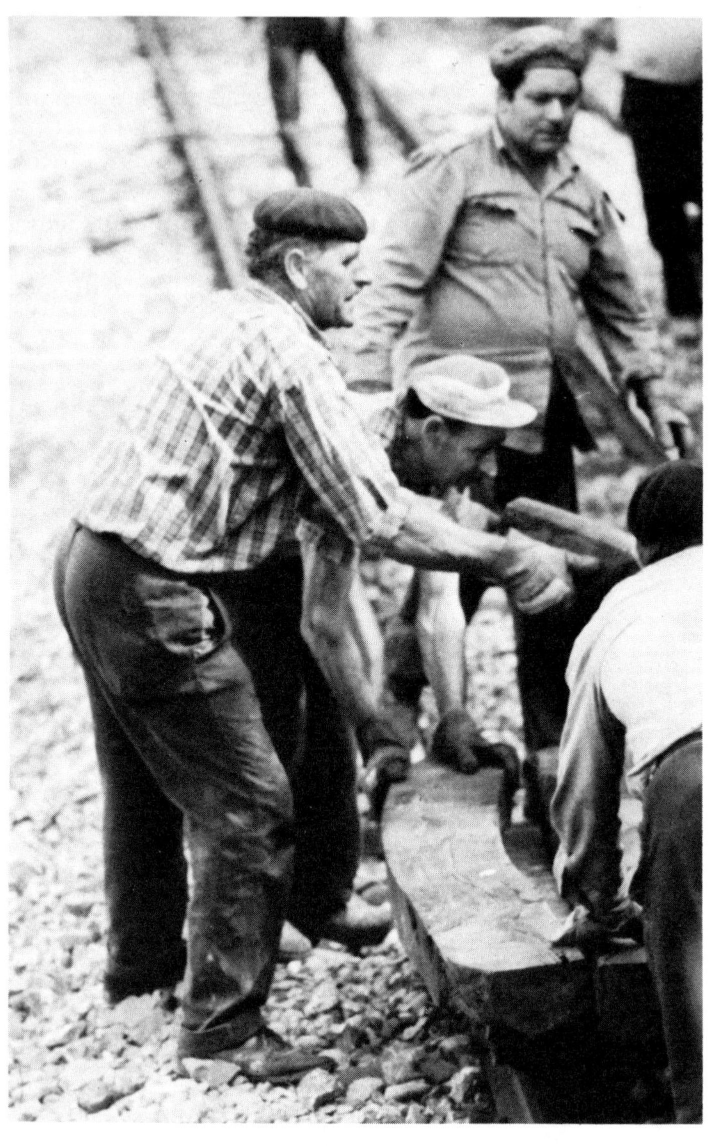

Railway worker, described in the text, repairing a rail line between Genoa and Casella, Italy. Little machinery and much muscle were utilized here. Taken with a 135 mm lens; 1/250 sec. at f/5.6.

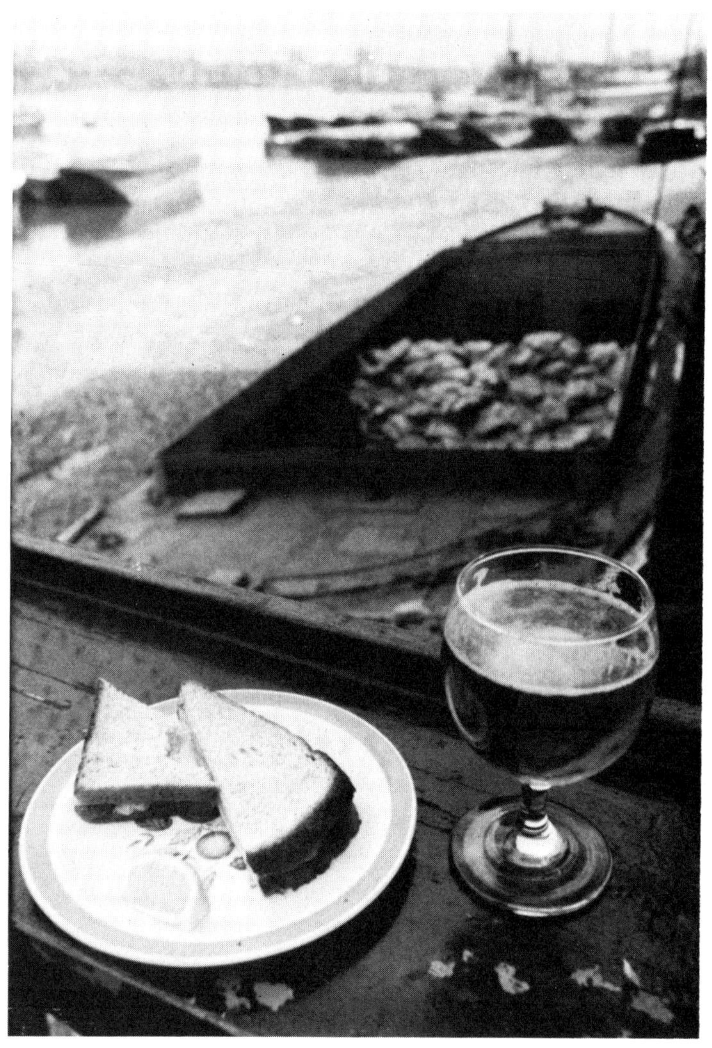

When you are sitting in a beautiful spot with your lunch before you, make a picture of it, as was done here with a glass of beer and a salmon sandwich (minus one bite). The picture was made on an outdoor lounge overlooking the River Thames at the May-flower Pub in Rotherhithe, near London, with a 50 mm lens; 1/125 sec. at f/16.

Shoot Your Lunch

There are people who go out in the morning and hunt or fish for their lunch. This involves time and skill but the reward is a freshly caught meal to enjoy. What we're suggesting here is a little different. When you are traveling, eat a big breakfast, a very light lunch (since this takes up valuable shooting time), and in the evening, when the light is gone, a nice dinner.

Try to find a spot for lunch that in itself is good picture material. While you are enjoying your meal, you can make a still life picture of it in an attractive setting. Many sidewalk cafes offer first-class scenery, as do mountaintop restaurants and pubs with outdoor decks overlooking water. The accompanying picture shows a beer and a salmon sandwich—minus one bite—with the River Thames at low tide in the background. This is one of the loveliest ways to enjoy a meal.

Signs

If you want one way of adding special interest to pictures, the careful use of unusual, colorful, and amusing signs is a good topic to include. Keep your eyes open for them. They are everywhere and you will eventually have to edit some out before you find yourself using more film than is really called for on this particular subject.

You may be required to photograph a building that is not, in itself, a thing of beauty. By positioning yourself right, you may be able to include an unusual sign in the foreground, thus drawing attention away from the structure itself. By using a wide-angle lens, you can keep both sign and building in focus, but the sign will appear even larger than it would with a normal lens. While you are walking, you will encounter many lovely old signs, some of which have become nearly illegible through age. Hand-painted ones can be very funny, especially if the sign-maker began to run out of space as he progressed from left to right. Sometimes it's the lettering—or the lack thereof—

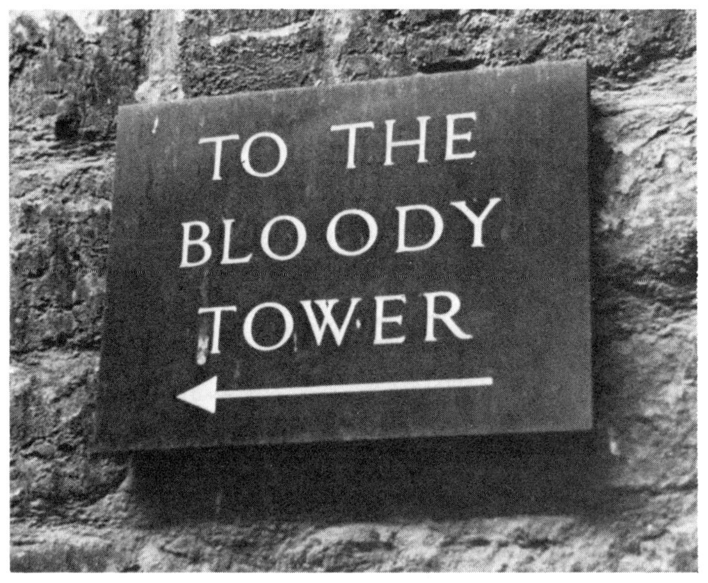

*No explanation is needed for this picture, which
was obviously made at the Tower of London.
Taken with a 50 mm lens; 1/125 sec. at f/16.*

that may be interesting. Other times, the colors will attract
your attention. Signs in other alphabets can add a foreign
flavor to your pictures, but don't overdo this idea.

What a sign says is often less important than how it
looks. A highly polished nameplate on a lovely old door
can be a picture in itself. What the sign says is unimpor-
tant compared with how it looks.

In some parts of the world, signs have no printing or
lettering. Instead, they display only a picture or a symbol
which is enough to tell the viewer what he wants to know.
A four-foot-long grasshopper in gold leaf may be advertis-
ing a bank.

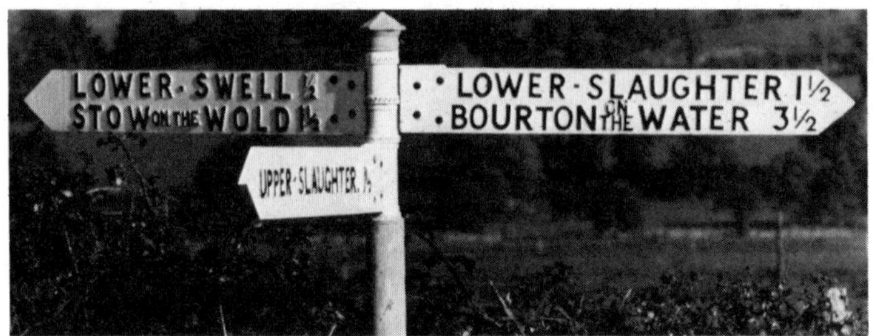

Take lots of interesting signs on your trip. This one in the English Cotswolds tells the story in a glimpse. Note the lush countryside, somewhat out of focus in the background. Taken with a 50 mm lens; 1/125 sec. at f/11.

Automobiles

If you're a car buff and you see a magnificent old auto on the road, get after it for pictures. Close-up pictures showing details of these vintage cars will be great in your finished collection of travel pictures. A brass company nameplate or headlamp, a fancy hood ornament, a bulb-type horn, or a shot of the unusual bodywork—this is what makes car photography interesting. Try also to get a picture of the driver and/or passengers.

Sleek new foreign cars might also be worth shooting for the car fans back home, especially if the cars are rare in your country. You may have an opportunity to visit the test tracks of certain manufacturers and watch the research vehicles going through their paces. This is an invitation for great action photographs, and it should not be passed up.

Boats

Try to imagine all the different sorts of boats and ships in the world. The subject is nearly endless. Look for different boats to photograph. A naggar on the Nile is quite different from anything we might be accustomed to. So is a Venetian gondola or a Chinese junk. Old Japanese fishing boats are made from huge pieces of rough-hewn lumber

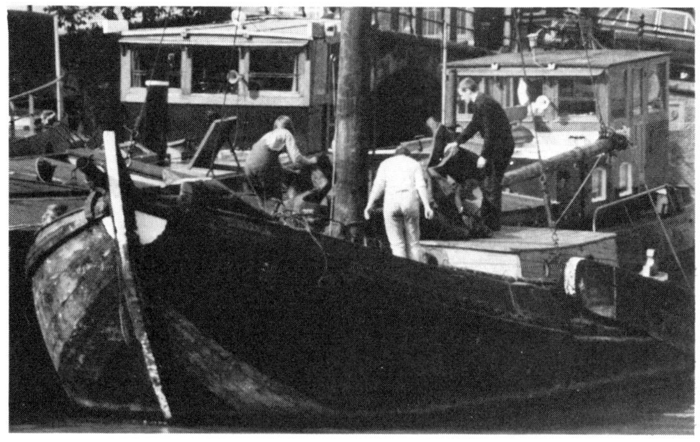

An old Dutch sailing barge being readied for a trip by a group of young people. These boats are really something to see when under way, with russet-colored sails filled and sideboards lowered for lateral stability. Taken with a 135 mm lens; 1/250 sec. at f/16.

and are held together with straps of iron. What picture possibilities these ancient designs present.

Coming into a lock on the River Thames, we saw a wood-fired steam riverboat, a little mahogany and brass beauty probably built around the turn of the century, and kept in perfect running order. The lockmaster pointed it out. "Watch that little one come out of the lock when I open the gates," he said. All the time the lock was filling, this little steamer was building up a head of steam. When the gate did open, "Whoop!" went the little whistle—and off she went, way ahead of the other boats in the lock. The family dog was there to oversee the pilot's work.

Another interesting boat, found throughout the waterways of the Netherlands, is the sailing barge. These are quite large and have russet-colored sails; instead of a keel or centerboard, they have sideboards which can be lowered for lateral stability. With one of these and a windmill in the distance, your picture will be a prototype for a Dutch ceramic tile.

Trees

Trees may seem an unusual—and rather dull—subject for a book on travel photography. However, you'll find them wherever you go, and you will want to include them often in your compositions. If you look back at your favorite pictures, you will certainly find trees prominently placed in many of them.

Seek out a few special types when you travel; they are really worth including in your pictures. One shot of an acacia tree says Africa at a glance. A Lombardy poplar instantly sets the stage for northern Italy. In the Orient, there are some trees that can't be found anywhere else. In western Europe, farmers have learned to position single or small groups of trees on their land to provide shade for their animals. They also know instinctively that these trees, along with the hedgerows and the varicolored fields, provide a natural beauty that cannot be surpassed.

The next time you see a tree, look at it objectively and try to appreciate its beauty. There are few lovelier forms in nature.

Reflections

Unless you have booked a three-week tour of the Sahara Desert, wherever you travel you will see water. And you can expect some fine reflections in that water. In still water, photograph mirror images; use moving water for brightly colored patterns that will make a good picture great.

Reflections in the canals of the Netherlands add a feeling of tranquillity to the scenes. In the little Italian seaports, reflections of the pastel-colored buildings make the water look like finger paintings. In the accompanying picture, the reflection of the church in a river in England repeats an already lovely scene—but this time a few ducks break the static composition and add a new element to the already handsome view.

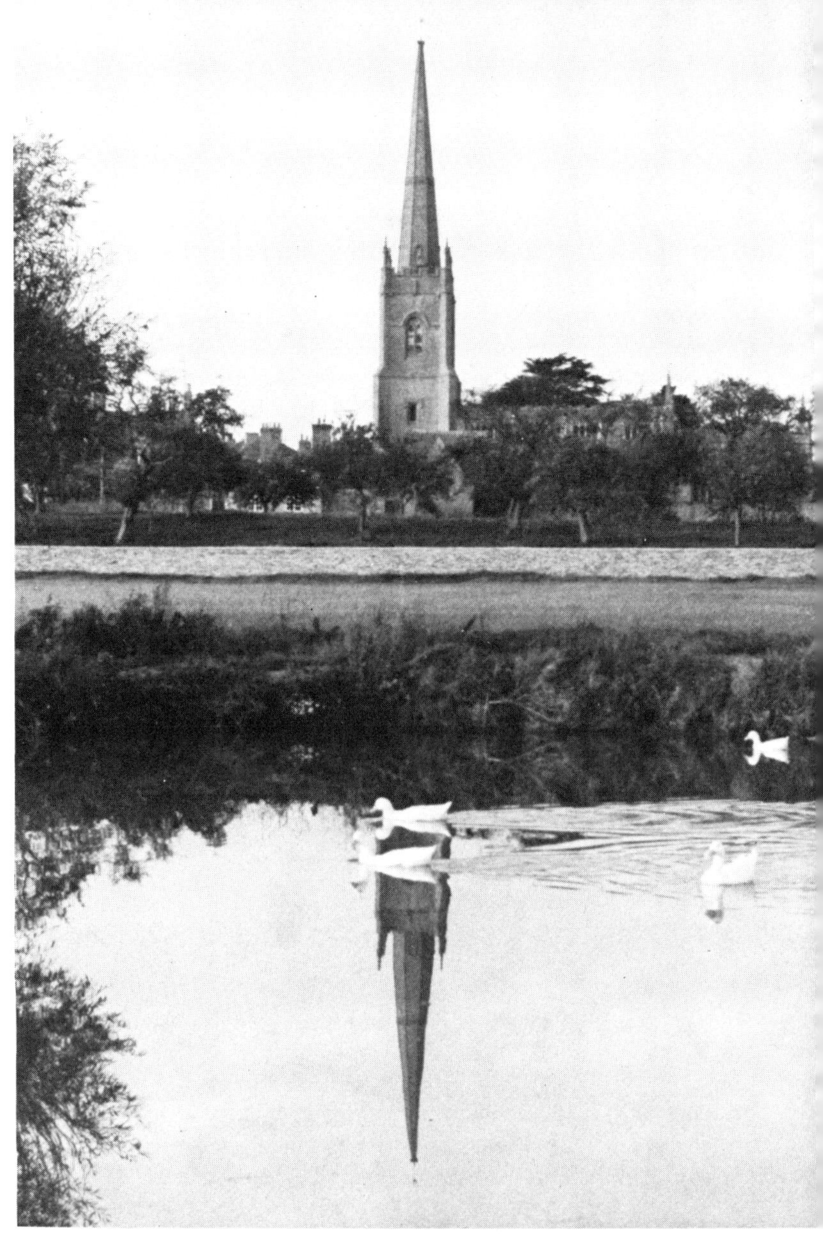

When you are set to shoot a reflection picture, wait to see if you can find some way to make it a little more interesting. The photographer saw these ducks heading into the scene and waited for this out-of-the-ordinary shot. The church is in Lechlade near the source of the River Thames, in England. Taken near sunset with a 50 mm lens; 1/125 sec. at f/4.

The setting sun reflected in the windows of an English pub makes the building appear on fire. The rest of the picture is a twilight blue color (see the color section). If you can find old windows made of irregular glass, you can pick up reflections of the scene behind you, distorted but beautiful. Brightly polished metal can give off reflections that make your pictures jump right up at the viewer.

Then there are reflections you don't want to picture. If you remembered to bring along your polarizing filter, don't forget to use it. When shooting with an SLR camera, merely place the polarizer on the lens and rotate it until the unwanted reflection is minimized. It will never go away completely but you can play it down quite well. Should you want to photograph a pond full of fish which are visible to your eye but canceled out by the reflection of the sky on the surface of the water, the polarizer will do the job very nicely.

6

Home Again

CUSTOMS ON RE-ENTRY

Where did the time go? It seems like only yesterday you took off for points unknown. Now here you are, almost at the finish line.

Shortly after your plane is airborne for the flight home, a flight attendant will pass around the U.S. Customs Declaration Form which you must fill out. This is a simple form and you'll have no trouble with it at all.

You will be asked to itemize each purchase you have made on your trip, including camera equipment, along with its price in U.S. dollars. (Note: If you asked for receipts for all of your major purchases, your accounting will be made much easier.) Total the amount of these purchases at the bottom of the form and sign your name, attesting to the fact that, to the best of your knowledge, all the information you have given is correct. Try to be as accurate as possible; the Customs inspectors have a very good idea how much the types of things brought back by the average tourist are worth.

You'll be allowed a certain amount of free taxable purchases. If your total is more than this allowance, just pay the duty on the difference. More than likely, you will still come out ahead.

Having registered all of your camera equipment with Customs upon leaving the country, you should have no problem in that regard, providing you have kept the Certificate of Registration issued upon departure.

When you get off the plane, you first go through Immigration where you will be separated from non-citizens. You will be asked where you have been and for how long. Your passport will be checked to be sure that everything is in order. If you have been in any country where certain diseases are endemic, you will be asked to show proof of immunization.

Then, you pick up your bags at the baggage pickup and head for Customs.

At the Customs counters, you will be greeted by polite, highly professional people who are only interested in getting you through quickly and on your way with the least possible delay. You will be asked a few simple questions about what you are bringing home with you. At the same time, your luggage will be inspected neatly and efficiently. Occasionally a much more thorough search may be made by special inspectors, but in general this is not the case. Once you are through Customs, you are free to go where you will.

PROCESSING YOUR FILM

Until your developed film is returned, you will be understandably nervous about the results.

If you're going to have your color film processed commercially, send 25 percent of your film to the lab each day for four days. If you numbered your rolls as you shot them, make a good mix of rolls in each batch to be processed. This way, should there be problems with one of the batches, you will have a little of something from each place you visited on your trip.

If you're going to process your own slides or negatives, be extra cautious. Do a test roll first to be sure everything is working correctly. Take the phone off the hook and run your first tank of film through. Use exactly the same process you have always used; don't try anything

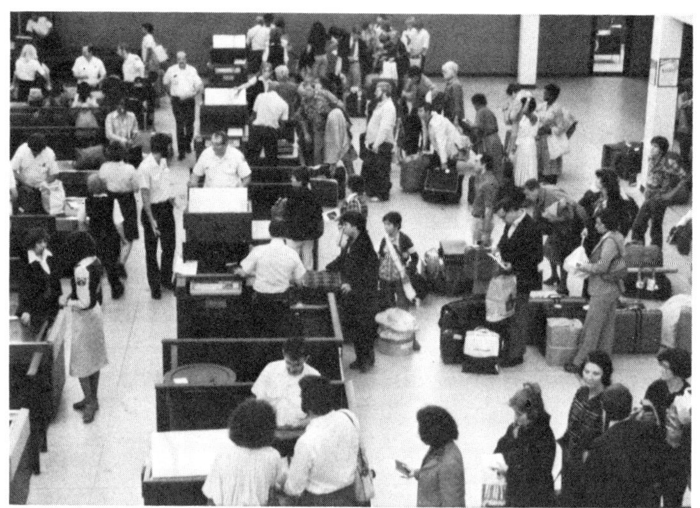

Here is the scene you can expect when you enter U. S. Customs on your way home. You always hope to sail through without a hitch. This picture was taken by available light, through glass from a waiting area upstairs, with a 50 mm lens; 1/30 sec. at f/2.8.

new now. By working carefully, you should turn out your film like clockwork.

Once the film is processed, most of your problems are behind you. When you begin to print, you can always correct your mistakes. The final business of editing is no problem compared to shooting and processing—and getting your photos safely back in your hands.

EDITING

Now comes the fun of it all. By making proof sheets of all your negatives, you are ready to go after your pictures in earnest.

Before anyone sees any of your slides or proof sheets, you must do your own editing. Nobody but you wants to see all the pictures you shot on your trip. The little time it takes to edit them down to a "show" or portfolio will be well spent. If you shot thirty 36-exposure rolls, you should be able to cut those 1,080 photos down to 100 or 200 really great pictures. Probably the hardest thing for a photographer to do is edit his or her own pictures; but it must be done.

If you are unable to cut your pile of pictures down any more than halfway, get in touch with somebody in your town who is an art director or professional photographer and ask him or her to run through your photos with you one time. Someone like this will knock your pictures down quickly—and painfully! You probably know what is really good just as well as the professional, but there is no sentiment involved in the professional's selection.

Best Shots

After you have narrowed your good shots down to a minimum, go back again and pick out perhaps a dozen which you consider your very best. Avoid such rationalizations as: "It was a little dark that day but this scene was just great—you should have been there!" The picture must stand alone on its merit, with no excuses necessary.

These are the pictures you should attempt to sell or publish. Perhaps one of them would make a good greeting card next holiday season.

People Pictures

The term "people pictures" applies to certain photographs that elicit a definite positive response; those pictures that, when shown, are always called "good" by viewers. By this, viewers don't mean the others are bad and that these are better, but that they really like these better. Oddly, the same pictures always seem to strike a chord when buried in a collection of work. They are crowd pleasers or show stoppers. There is no rational explanation for this; it is just a simple fact of life in the photographic world. Each of these pictures has an appeal to people that others don't have. The more "people pictures" you show, the better a photographer people will think you are.

As you continue to show your small selection of pictures, you may remove some "non-people" pictures and add a few new ones. Eventually, your portfolio will contain almost exclusively "people pictures." What you have done is merely allow the editors to do their work and then let them enjoy the fruits of their labor.

MARKETS FOR YOUR PICTURES

Here are a number of places to submit your pictures for viewing or publication.

Camera Clubs

First of all, if you are not already, you can become active in your local camera club. Those pictures you made on your trip should be enough to carry you for a long time in any camera club.

Newspapers

If you live in a small town, your local newspaper editor might be interested to look over a limited selection of your work for possible publication in his paper. You might even offer to write a short column about your trip; this could be supported by a couple of your pictures.

Pictures for newspapers must usually be black-and-white, preferably with very little grain. If you shot color negative film, making black-and-white prints on special panchromatic paper is not difficult. If you used slide film, you must have a black-and-white internegative made, from which you can make your own black-and-white prints.

Exhibitions

You might make up a selection of mounted prints of your best work and display them at your next local art fair. Art fairs are popular everywhere, and you might be quite successful. You might sell enough prints to at least pay for the film you used on your trip.

Publications

If you want to sell your work to magazines or book publishers, ask your local bookdealer to get you a copy of the latest *Photographer's Market* published annually by Writer's Digest. The book is fairly expensive, but it lists thousands of places where you can submit your photographs. To order directly, write to: Writer's Digest, 9933 Alliance Road, Cincinnati, OH 45242.

Note: Most of those markets are looking for black-and-white prints or for 35 mm or 2¼″ square color transparencies. Color prints are generally not acceptable. Also, for your own protection, do not send original transparencies. Have good duplicates made and send those; if a prospective buyer is interested but insists on originals, send them only on request.

Finally, you can just sit and enjoy your pictures yourself. Frame prints and hang them on the wall. Make albums. Show slides to local clubs. After all, the main object of your trip was enjoyment. Enjoy it—while you're there and after your return.

Appendix

Metric Conversion Information

When You Know	Multiply by	To Find
inches (in.)	25.4	millimetres (mm)
feet (ft.)	0.3048	metres (m)
miles (mi.)	1.609	kilometres (km)
ounces (oz.)	28.349	grams (g)
pounds (lbs.)	0.453	kilograms (kg)
pounds per square inch (psi.)	0.0703	kilograms per square centimetre (kg/sqcm)
cubic feet (cu. ft.)	0.0283	cubic meters
Fahrenheit temperature (F)	1.8 after subtracting 32	Celsius temperature (C)

ASA AND DIN FILM SPEEDS

ASA	DIN	ASA	DIN	ASA	DIN	ASA	DIN
6	9	25	15	100	21	400	27
8	10	32	16	125	22	500	28
10	11	40	17	160	23	640	29
12	12	50	18	200	24	800	30
16	13	64	19	250	25	1000	31
20	14	80	20	320	26	1250	32

Index

Aerials, 130-135
  basic rules for, 130
  preparation for, 134
Arc shooting, 45-46
Atmospheric haze, 96
Attitude, 56

Backlighting, 108
Baggage, 15-16
Black-and-white or color,
      16-17
Boats, 146-148
Bridges, 114-116
Buildings, 89
  converging lines, 51-54
  details of, 91-96
  normal focal length lens, 96
  short telephoto lens, 95
  wide-angle views, 95
Bullfight, 137

Calendar, travel, 14
Camera, new, 17
Camera clubs, 155
Camera equipment, 16-17
  carrying, 18-19
  packing, 17-18
Camera first aid, 27-28
Canal locks, 89
Canals, 88-89
Candids, 74-85
Castles and ruins, 105-107
Cathedrals, 104-105
Changing of the guard, 81
Checking out equipment
  batteries, 26
  dusting brush, 27
  mechanical linkage, 27
  shutter, 26-27
Children, 66-69
Cities, 89-119
Close-ups, 96-104

Close-up shots, 66
Collage, 99
Color negative film, 134, 135
Composition, 46-51
  best way to learn, 46
Contrived picture, 74
Countryside, 85-89
Cross-star filter, 108
Customs on re-entry, 151-152

Days per city, 14
Depth, illusion of, 96

Editing, 153-155
Equipment, checking out, 26-27
Excursion ticket, 15
Exhibitions, 156
Exposure control, 39

Farms, 88
File cards, 12
Filter, 80B conversion, 124, 135
Flash or strobe, 136
Flea markets, 99
Floater policy, 31
Flower markets, 107-108
Flying club, local, 133
Foreign customs, 35
Fountains, 108-109
Framing a scene, 89

Gadget bag, 19
  outfitting, 20-26
Gateways, 109

Haze filter, 134
Haze and fog, 121-122
High vantage points, 96
How much film?, 19
Humor, 70-74

Immigration, 35-36

Insurance, 30-32
Interiors, 116-117, 128-130
  wide-angle lens for, 129
Itinerary, 13-14

Landscapes, 85-88
London, rain list for, 13
Lunch, 144

Markets for your pictures,
  155-156
Mini-portfolio, 29-30
Movies or stills, 16
Museums, 128-129

Notes, 37
Newspapers, 155
Newsstand, 118
Night pictures, 122
  best time to take, 125
  special equipment for, 124

Overseas trip
  preparation for, 11-15
  three phases of, 9
  return from, 151

P.C. lenses, 52
Packing, 15-28
Parades, 81
People, 57-85, 154-155
  with tools, 88
Perspective control, 51
Photographer's Market, 156
Picture lists, 12-13
Places to see and photograph,
  12
Plan, next day's, 55-56
Points of interest, 104
Polarizing filter, 108, 150
Portraits, in rain, 128
Practice shooting, 28-30

Processing your film, 152-153
Publications, 156

Rain pictures, 125-128
  changing lenses in rain,
    125-127
  special equipment for, 125
Rainy day planning, 13
Reflections, 127, 148-150
Registration, certificate of,
    33-35
Reservations, 14-15
Restaurants, 12, 116, 144

Seascapes and harbors, 119-121
Shopping stops, 12
Shoot, what to, 57-150
Shooting, first day, 36
Short time exposures, 117
Shutter jam, 27-28
Signs, 144-146
Simplicity, 99
Soccer, 136
Special film shoulder bag, 19-20
Special situations, 121-139
Sports, 136
Statues, 109-114
Subject interest, 39-45
Sunrise, 120
Sunsets, 120

Telephoto lens, short, 66
Theatre pictures, 135-136
Time schedule, 13-14
Trains, 139-143
Trees, 148
Twilight, 125

White sky of a rainy day, 127

X-Ray at airports, 34-35